## Praise for *What We Say Matters*

*What We Say Matters* shows how speech can be a spiritual practice. A language of the heart has the power to create a world of connection, peace, and compassion in our own lives and in the whole human family. I am excited and inspired by how Judith and Ike present the NVC principles from the context of yoga philosophy and Buddhism in a way that is simple, clear, and practical, yet filled with depth and wisdom. I highly and enthusiastically recommend this book.

—John Kinyon, trainer and mediator, The Center for Nonviolent Communication

As a longtime student of NVC (thanks to Judith and Ike), I am grateful for the clarity and wisdom of the material presented in *What We Say Matters*. I was inspired and encouraged by their personal stories and am excited to experiment with the practical suggestions and exercises. When I imagine the people who will read and use this book, I feel hopeful that we can all contribute to creating a more peaceful world.

—Marcia Miller, co-owner of Yoga on High, Columbus, OH

When I read Judith and Ike's book, I feel happy, as though I have friends who speak to me and for me (rather than *at* me or *down* to me), and who will coach and counsel me through the intricacies of communicating more clearly and carefully, heart to heart, so

that we may flower in each other's presence. Thank you for this offering, a treasure that helps me to unfold inside.

—Edward Brown, Zen teacher, author of *The Tassajara Bread Book* and *The Complete Tassajara Cookbook*

This book reminds me of conversations around the dinner table at Judith and Ike's house, exploring ways to deepen our consciousness and more fully live this one precious life. Now everyone is invited to be at that table.

—Kit Miller, Director/Celebrator, Bay Area Nonviolent Communication

# What We Say Matters

By Judith Hanson Lasater

Published by Rodmell Press

*Relax and Renew*

*Living Your Yoga*

*30 Essential Yoga Poses*

*Yoga for Pregnancy*

*Yoga Abs*

*A Year of Living Your Yoga*

*Yogabody*

By Judith Hanson Lasater and Ike K. Lasater

Published by Rodmell Press

*What We Say Matters*

By Ike K. Lasater

Published by PuddleDancer Press

*Words That Work in Business*

# What We Say Matters:

## *Practicing Nonviolent Communication*

Judith Hanson Lasater, Ph.D., P.T.

Ike K. Lasater, J.D., M.C.P.

RODMELL PRESS
BERKELEY, CALIFORNIA ▾ 2009

*What We Say Matters: Practicing Nonviolent Communication,*
copyright © 2009 by Judith Hanson Lasater, Ph.D., P.T,
and Ike K. Lasater, J.D., M.C.P. All rights reserved.

No part of this book may be reproduced or transmitted in
any form or by any means, electronic or mechanical, including
photocopying, recording, or by an information storage or
retrieval system, without written permission from Rodmell Press,
2147 Blake St., Berkeley, CA 94704-2715; (510) 841-3123,
(510) 841-3191 (fax), www.rodmellpress.com.

Library of Congress Cataloging-in-Publication Data
is available.

Printed and bound in China
First edition
ISBN-10: 1-930485-24-7
ISBN-13: 978-1-930485-24-2
13 12 11 10 09 1 2 3 4 5 6 7 8 9 10

Editor: Linda Cogozzo
Associate Editor: Holly Hammond
Indexer: Ty Koontz
Design: Gopa & Ted2, Inc.
Lithographer: Kwong Fat Offset Printing Co., Ltd.
Judith Author Photo: Elizabeth Lasater
Ike Author Photo: Melissa Walker-Scott
Text set in Palatino LT Standard 9.8/17.4

Distributed by Publishers Group West

For our children and their loved ones

# Contents

Acknowledgments xiii

Introduction: Why We Wrote This Book 1

1. Satya and Right Speech 7

2. Nonviolent Communication 13

3. Four Communication Choices 35

4. Listening to Ourselves and Others 57

5. What We Say Matters 69

6. Talking to Our Partners 85

7. Talking to Our Children and Parents 101

8. Talking at Work 117

9. Talking in the World 137

Resources 145

About the Authors 149

From the Publisher 153

Index 155

*A new idea is first condemned as ridiculous,*
*and then dismissed as trivial, until finally*
*it becomes what everybody knows.*

—William Blake

# Acknowledgments

WE WISH TO THANK the people who inspired us, taught us, and supported us as we wrote this book. Marshall Rosenberg, Ph.D., was the catalyst who helped us to see how *satya* and right speech could be lived, as we observed his practice and teaching of Nonviolent Communication. Our three children and our daughter-in-law have all given us great reason to become more aware of speech and how we could use it to create connection and clarity in our relationships. Finally, we wish to acknowledge all of our teachers, including B.K.S. Iyengar and Charlotte Joko Beck. To all of these people, we are humbly grateful.

Judith wishes to thank her yoga students and her friend and Zen teacher, Linda Cutts Weintrab, for their constancy. Ike would like to thank his teachers and colleagues on the road to incorporating the skills and understanding of Nonviolent Communication into his day-to-day life. In particular, he wants to thank John

Kinyon for his support and companionship in the adventure of learning to mediate using NVC and learning how to offer trainings for others to do the same. We both thank Julie Stiles for her keen eye, sensitive review, and helpful editing in the writing stages of this book, and special appreciation for her collaboration with Ike in the creation of chapter 9.

We also thank our publishers, Donald Moyer and Linda Cogozzo, for their vision and for their practical help as this book took shape.

# Introduction: Why We Wrote This Book

*Speech is a mirror of the soul:*
*as a man speaks, so is he.*
— PUBLILIUS SYRUS

"THAT'S NOT A FEELING," my husband Ike stated, gazing at me across the kitchen with a mixture of excitement and smugness. My look back at him was less than pleased. He had just returned from a seminar with Marshall Rosenberg on Nonviolent Communication (NVC), and he was telling me that my words did not describe "feelings" according to what he had learned. Unfortunately I was unable to hear his excitement or appreciate his insight, because I was too busy reacting negatively to him "telling me how to talk."

When we tell this story at the NVC seminars that we teach together, we offer it as a perfect example of how not to practice the principles we share in this book. But the difficulty we had with each other was nothing compared with what happened as we began to "use" this technique with our three teenagers. We laugh now, but it was a painful period, as first Ike and then I began to change something we thought we already knew how to do: communicate.

Speech is the most human of activities. Babies begin making sounds from birth to communicate their needs, and a child's first word is a cause for celebration. Speech allows for the functioning of society on all levels. It would seem that nothing could be more natural than the use of speech to express our needs and to respond to the needs of others.

But belying its simple appearance, speech is actually created out of a complex interplay of factors. Our thoughts, beliefs, and perceptions powerfully shape our language to reflect our particular world. Without a clear awareness of our words, we can be dumbfounded daily by interactions that result in the opposite of what we intended. Research tells us that only a small percentage of what we say is actually heard, and even less of that is actually understood. Add to this the fact that different languages express actions and thoughts with different structures, and it is a wonder we understand each other at all.

Our interest in communication began much earlier than that incident in the kitchen in 1997. We both began to study yoga in 1970 and learned about the eight limbs, or *ashtanga* principles, of the yoga philosophy presented by Patanjali in the Yoga Sutra. The first principle for the practice of yoga is called *yama*, meaning "restraint." There are five restraints, the first and most important of which is *ahimsa*, or nonviolence. Another yama is *satya*, or truth. The practitioner is admonished to speak the truth or, more accurately, to restrain from speech that is not true.

Ike and I both found that this ancient advice to speak the truth raised many questions. Whose truth? Don't we all experience reality differently? In the book *Life Strategies*, Phillip McGraw states, "There is no reality, only perception." Ike and I found that while we agreed with truth as a value, we were not as easily able to understand it as a practice, as something we did with each utterance.

Throughout the years, we also became interested in Buddhist meditation and took up a daily practice of sitting in the Zen tradition. As with yoga philosophy, we found that Buddhism offered us a list of precepts, one of which is "right speech," or using speech in a way that does not harm oneself or others—very much like satya. Again, we agreed in principle but were a little baffled about how to practice it, other than to consciously not tell lies.

One day at a Buddhist retreat, Ike was almost casually introduced to the basic principles of Nonviolent Communication and, in the way of so many things, before long he found himself in a workshop with Dr. Rosenberg, the founder of the method. Soon I joined Ike in the study of NVC. All I remember of the first couple of years was that I didn't get it at all. We both just tried to focus on the most basic structures from the technique, and slowly, over time, we began to integrate the work into our lives. What helped us most was simply practice. Lots of practice.

We organized a regular weekly practice group at our house and tried to practice with each other every day at home. We joked that we lived in an "NVC ashram." We took seminars, some as long as ten days, to immerse ourselves in NVC. And we finally realized that what we were doing was learning a foreign language, the language of empathy and compassion.

We found an interesting interplay between the conscious practice of meditation and yoga asana and the conscious choice of words. Dr. Rosenberg's approach felt familiar to us, as we attempted to bring our practices off the meditation cushion and yoga mat and into our lives as spouses, parents, teachers, and citizens.

The thesis of this book is that what we say matters—that is, when we speak, we change the world. Blending the spiritual awareness of the power of speech into the actualizing technique of Nonviolent Communication creates a powerful tool for affecting not only our lives and the lives of those around us but also the world at large. Without awareness of the power of our language, we continue to reinforce the patterns, both emotional and psychological, that contribute to our suffering and the suffering of others.

Using speech as a spiritual practice is the act and art

of bringing a deeper awareness to our words so they not only connect us with ourselves but also reflect what is truly alive in us. When we do this, we help create the kind of world we want to live in and leave to future generations, because then our words promote life.

We now know that learning NVC needn't be so difficult. We finally feel that we are beginning to understand satya and right speech in ways we never thought possible. It has taken us years to understand that the first thing that must happen if we are to practice spiritual speech is an internal shift in awareness. From that initial shift, our language then begins to shift without conscious effort to reflect on the outside what has already happened inside. When these two shifts occur, we are more likely to enjoy our interactions with others.

We wrote *What We Say Matters* to share with you what we learned about how to approach this work. The book is organized into nine chapters. We begin by discussing satya, right speech, and NVC itself. Then we explore the principles of NVC in how we talk to ourselves, our partners, our children and parents, and at the workplace. Each chapter includes practices intended to help you take NCV deeply into your life. To help you do so, consider:

- keeping a journal of specific phrases or sentences that have helped or not helped you connect with yourself and others, or of your other practice experiences;
- asking a friend to be your empathy buddy, to help you approach a difficult conversation;

- forming a weekly *What We Say Matters* study group.

Our continued learning has created effects that have been nothing short of miraculous in our lives. We are so happy you are joining us in this adventure. We hope that some of these techniques will help you speak in a way that meets your needs for clarity and ease, and the world's need for compassion.

# 1 Satya and Right Speech

*Is sloppiness in speech caused by ignorance or apathy? I don't know and I don't care.*

—WILLIAM SAFIRE

THE ANCIENT TEACHINGS of yoga and Buddhism have many things in common. They both evolved from the Hindu culture, they both contain techniques that teach us how to live a life of fulfillment free from suffering, and they both offer teachings specifically about speech and its importance in our lives.

The Yoga Sutra of Patanjali, the ancient sourcebook delineating the psychology and practice of yoga, offers two sutra (verses) on the subject of speech. The first is in chapter (or *pada*) II, verse 30. Here Patanjali lists the five *yamas*, or restraints, that are recommended for the practitioner of yoga. These restraints are *ahimsa* (nonharming), *satya* (truth), *asteya* (nonstealing), *brahmacharya* (chastity), and *aparigraha* (nongreed). The second mention of satya is in pada II, verse 36. Georg Feuerstein translates this (in *The Yoga-Sutra of Patanjali*): "When grounded in truthfulness, action (and its) fruition depend (on him)." This means that as we practice satya on deeper and deeper levels, whatever we say is an accurate reflection of reality. This verse could also mean that when we are grounded in the state of yoga, the state of pure being, then we cannot say anything that is not the truth, and so anything we say is true. It is not true because we have made something come true, but rather because there is no separation between our consciousness, the truth, and what we speak.

There are, however, other aspects to the practice of truth. All yamas, including satya, are considered to be secondary to the expression of ahimsa, or nonharming. I (Judith) understand that we can never "tell the truth" if we ignore the foundational practice of nonharming.

In the Yoga Sutra, satya is offered in the context of a restraint. This means that we are to consciously hold back speech that will be harmful. It is thus implied that we remain aware of all speech, so that words that are not truthful, and therefore harmful, are avoided. Importantly, no instruction is given in the Yoga Sutra about what we are to say or how we are to speak. Instead, Patanjali exhorts the practitioner about what to avoid.

The Buddhist eightfold path offers teachings similar to those found in yoga. The eight practices are divided into three sections. The first section is about wisdom and includes right understanding and right thought. The second section is about ethical conduct and includes right speech, right action, and right livelihood. The final section is about mental discipline and includes right effort, right mindfulness, and right concentration.

Right speech is speech that furthers the practice of the speaker and contributes to the well-being of others and the world. Right speech is therefore intentional speech that rejects mindless chatter, gossip, slander, and lies. When we are honest with ourselves, self-reflection often reveals that much of our speech is harmful at worst and unnecessary at best.

The practice of right speech is just as difficult to apply as the practice of satya. Both teachings describe what to do, but neither gives much guidance on how to do it. Additionally, there is no way to measure if one has "done" right speech or satya. I can know when I have practiced the *asana* (posture) of Salamba Sirsasana (Headstand), but whether I have practiced right speech or satya is pure judgment.

Nonviolent Communication can thus be a boon to practitioners of satya or right speech. The techniques of NVC are first and most importantly about inner awareness. Then NVC offers specific ways to consider and practice speech. Like yoga and Buddhism, NVC considers speech to be very powerful. This power is twofold.

First, there is power in paying attention to how I phrase what I say. The way I phrase a thought to myself before I speak, expresses how I think and what I believe about the world. One of my favorite sayings is: My words reflect my thoughts, my thoughts reflect my beliefs, and my beliefs, especially the unexamined ones, run my world.

To consider this in the opposite way, whatever unexamined thoughts I have are going to shape how I act and how I interact with others. They will determine how others see me and how they treat me. For example, if I tell myself through my thoughts that I am worthless, I will begin to act that way, and others will treat me as if that were the truth.

The heart of any spiritual practice begins with remembering at all times to be present with my inner states. This remembrance is crucial, because it is the foundation for understanding this important teaching: *I am not my thoughts*. I have thoughts, but they are a manifestation of my being and are not who I am. One of the best ways to remember that I am not my thoughts is to cultivate the habit of being present first with myself and then with my speech, both internal and external. The way I say things reifies my beliefs, especially the belief that I am my thoughts.

An example of this is that we sometimes say the opposite of what we mean. I might feel hurt because you did not arrive for our date on time. But instead of saying that, I say, "I guess you don't care about our relationship." This statement is not likely to get me the connection I want, and it might even start a fight.

# Nonviolent Communication 2

*The three most important mantras are:*
*Tell the truth. Tell the truth. Tell the truth.*
—JUDITH HANSON LASATER

THE FIRST TIME I (Judith) took a seminar on Nonviolent Communication from Marshall Rosenberg, I spent a lot of time squirming in my seat. It wasn't that I didn't like what he was saying; it was that I couldn't understand how to do it myself.

As Dr. Rosenberg had conversations with various people in the workshop, one by one they would laugh, cry, or both, as they felt the power of connection with him. "How does he do that?" I thought. It seemed like he was working magic. I couldn't begin to explain what he was doing; I just knew I wanted to be able to use my words in the same compassionate way. Years later, with more training under my belt, I have a deeper understanding of how NVC can be a practical application of satya and right speech.

In the early stages of learning NVC, it can seem to be all about word order and choice—syntax—and in this book we focus most of our attention on these aspects. But bear in mind that NVC is fundamentally about *intention.* Syntax is just a strategy to remind us of our intention.

The underlying intention in using NVC is to connect: to connect with ourselves first and only then to attempt to connect with others. Out of this connection, we can create mutually satisfying outcomes. The words we use will change, based on the situation or subculture in which we find ourselves. Therefore we hope you will use words that have both meaning and resonance for the person you are talking with.

The practice of being connected with yourself in a visceral, noncognitive way is powerful. We are unlikely to connect to another human being unless we are connected with our own needs. This is not something most of us are taught as children, and generally it takes time and practice to develop the skill. In fact, as children we are sometimes actually taught to deny our own needs.

Have you ever heard a parent tell a young child, "No, you don't want that vase," as the curious child reaches for Grandmother's precious art piece? The statement is not true; the child definitely wants the vase in order to fulfill a need for learning or perhaps for fun. The child is actually being told, "You can't touch the vase." From these little life experiences, we are being taught that what we think we want is not really what we want. No wonder then that when we are forty-five years old and sitting in an NVC seminar, we are flummoxed and confused when someone asks us to identify our needs.

As part of the conditioning process, as we lose touch with our own needs, we learn to protect ourselves from criticism, avoid punishment, and redirect blame. Learning to connect at the level of needs is a way of learning to step out of our habitual ways of reacting. As you identify, time and time again, what needs were and were not met by your actions in a situation, particularly one where you reacted habitually, the possibility opens up to act differently in the future. In this way, you can use NVC to change how you relate to yourself and others.

When you make it a practice to connect with your needs, you shift into learning mode. For example, your coworker is complaining again that your boss never listens to anyone. You could ignore his comment or agree with it, or you could silently translate his statement into an expression of his own needs. Perhaps he wants to be seen or heard or appreciated. Once I hear my coworker's statement as a statement of his needs instead of as a statement about someone else, I notice a different reaction in myself. I then have the opportunity to respond directly to his needs instead of responding from my reaction. If you do find yourself reacting instead of responding, you might inquire into the need you were seeking to meet by your reaction, as well as what needs of yours were not met by the interaction.

The natural result of this inquiry is the question, How might I do it differently next time, in order to better meet my needs? We encourage you to do this inquiry without a sense of judgment, punishment, blame, shame, self-condemnation, or guilt. Just simply inquire about what needs were and were not met and what might be ways to better meet them. Thus inquiry, which is at the heart of the practices of yoga and Buddhist meditation, can be brought into our daily interactions and activities.

When you practice this inquiry, you learn to become aware. You mourn and celebrate your conduct, building from what you liked and shifting away from what you didn't like, all in order to better meet your needs. Soon you begin to remember, when you are in a moment of agitation, to try a new choice. Then you learn from that choice. The natural consequence of this process is that you learn skills that are in alignment with meeting your needs and the needs of others.

Thus, from our perspective, at the core of NVC is not only developing the skills and practicing them but also gaining experience in choosing new possibilities based on needs, instead of repeating habitual patterns. By being connected with our own needs, our intention is clarified moment by moment. This is speech as a spiritual practice.

## An NVC Primer: The Basic Concepts

There are four basic steps in learning to use NVC. These steps are meant to be used not as a formula but as a launching pad. Holding tightly to these four steps can disconnect you from the present moment and can stand in the way of clear and true communication. So start with these four steps but be willing to move beyond them as you feel more at home with the process.

**Step 1: Make observations.** To make an observation is to report on what we commonly call the facts. The Yoga Sutra calls this *pramana* (pada I, v. 7). Some observations are: "The month is August" or "John arrived at noon."

"John arrived late" is not an observation; it is a judgment. Why? Because John may not believe that he is late, and if Mary tells him he is late, he might deny it and argue the contrary. Perhaps in John's belief system, ten or fifteen minutes is not really late, whereas Mary maintains that even one minute past the agreed upon time is late. An observation would be: "John arrived ten minutes past the time Mary remembers him agreeing to arrive."

It is important to make this distinction because when we use judgments in our conversations with others, we tend to get off track and begin arguing about what is true—in this case, whether or not John was late. Such an argument probably will not get to the heart of how

John and Mary would like to be together. What might be true is that Mary was worried about John's safety, while John was happy that he was feeling so relaxed about this time with Mary. Instead of enjoying each other, they might spend their time together at odds with each other.

That John was late or not late is what I (Judith) call a pseudo fact—a judgment masquerading as a fact. Some common pseudo facts are "You are driving too fast" or "It is really cold in here" or "That was a really good movie." I call these pseudo facts because at first these statements sound like simple observations, but in fact they are not. In Thomas Byrom's translation of *The Dhammapada*, Buddha is quoted as saying, "Do not seek enlightenment; merely cease to cherish beliefs." Our opinions and beliefs are pseudo facts. A pseudo fact is "It's hot in this room." It is asserted as a fact, but it is indeed a judgment. Another person could say, "No, it's not. I'm cold." An observation would be (looking at a thermometer): "It's 80 degrees in this room." This statement is not likely to become the crux of an argument.

Imagine the following. A parent knocks and enters the bedroom of a teenager with the following words: "This room is a mess. Please clean it up by tomorrow morning because company is coming." We almost guarantee that the response from the teenager will be: "It's not a mess." If the parent persists, the teenager will likely switch to, "But I like it this way." And if that fails, the teenager will resort to the time-honored, "Whose room is it anyway?" We would bet lots of money that what follows from these interchanges is not a period of sweet connection between parent and child.

A more desirable connection is likely to result if the interchange begins with observation language. Pay attention to how different you feel when you imagine the communication starting with, "When I see your clothes on the floor, dishes with food on them on your desk, and your bed unmade . . ." The key point here is to notice the difference between making an observation and making a judgment. For example, to say, "When I see that your room is a mess . . ." is not to make an observation. The term "mess" is a judgment; messes are not desirable. (More on the teenage bedroom drama to come.)

Observation used in this way is an expression of what we call spiritual speech. It is learning to leave out our judgments and beliefs *about* what is observed and just describe it as a camera would record it. Later in this chapter, we offer practice exercises to help you to refine your awareness of observations versus judgments.

We are not proposing a new set of rights and wrongs. It is not wrong to use judgments. We just want you to be aware of using them, so you can learn what ensues from using judgments and what ensues from using observations instead. Then the choice is yours.

The judgments at issue here are moralistic opinions about someone or something being right or wrong. We will never be able to do away with evaluating whether our needs are being met or not. That is a form of judgment. But in making that evaluation, we are not condemning anyone for their motives.

**Step 2: Name your feelings.** Feelings are emotions and are connected to bodily sensations. Feelings are constantly changing and constantly arising. They tell us simply whether our needs have been met or unmet in that moment. In that sense, feelings are "flares" from the unconscious that alert us to the state of our needs: met or unmet.

For example, we might feel happy, content, at ease, connected to self and others, or full of energy. These feelings tell us that we are perceiving that our needs are being met in that moment. Or we might feel sad, lonely, afraid, irritated, or confused. These feelings tell us that we are interpreting and therefore believing that our needs are not being met in the moment.

All human beings have feelings, and they are constantly arising and changing. If you don't believe that, get married and have kids! Feelings are signals shooting from the depths of the unconscious mind, alerting us that we need to pay attention. In that way, feelings are like a yoga pose. When we bend forward in Uttanasana (Standing Forward Bend) and feel lots of stretch in the hamstring muscles at the back of the upper thigh, attention is immediately brought there. The sensation is telling us to pay attention to the hamstrings and how they need some release. This act of paying attention is the practice. Spiritual practice is not the asana but the act of noticing during the practice of the asana. Part of the benefit of a regular asana practice is to remind us to pay attention. Feelings serve the same purpose.

If we learn the habit of paying attention to feelings as they arise, we are immediately brought into the present moment. And this is the hallmark of spiritual practice. You cannot simultaneously be paying attention to your feelings and be lost in thoughts about the situation. Being lost in thoughts is our suffering.

One important thing to remember is that, according to the NVC model, feelings arise separately from what other people say and do. Others might stimulate my feelings, but my feelings are mine and are unique to how I experience the world. One person might feel sad from hearing something on the news, while another might feel happy upon hearing the same thing. The difference lies in the individual, not in the news. The news does not create feelings, although it may very well stimulate feelings. There is a difference.

Let's say that you and I go to a movie. You cry during the movie and I don't. The observation is that we both saw a movie. The stimulus was the same for both of us. We reacted differently, based upon our unique makeup. Our makeup comes with us from the womb and is shaped by our life experiences, particularly the patterns formed in early childhood.

Another thing to remember is that to say, "I feel like you are a pain in the neck" is not to express a feeling.

What is being stated is an opinion. Many people use the word "feeling" to express beliefs, thoughts, and images. To say, "I feel like you were acting unfairly" is not expressing a feeling; it is analyzing how you acted. If instead you said, "When I heard what you said to me, I felt sad," you would be using observation language ("When I heard what you said") followed by feeling language ("I felt sad"). This use of language brings the speaker back to her own truth. It is what occurs when we observe thoughts arising in meditation. We predict that you will enjoy the responses you receive when you do not mix the expression of feelings with analysis or opinion.

Finally, remember that "feelings" as used in NVC do not include those that involve another person. For example, "I feel abandoned" involves another person. It takes another person to abandon me. Instead I could say, "I feel lonely and afraid." Those feelings may have arisen when the other person left.

Try saying these two sentences out loud. First, "You abandoned me." That expresses a belief about someone's behavior. Upon hearing that sentence, the other person may feel that he is being judged. He may even say, "I didn't abandon you," and you might respond with, "Oh, yes you did," and an argument could ensue. Now say aloud, "When you left the house, I felt lonely and afraid." The other person cannot argue with your feelings of being lonely and afraid, because they are yours and are alive in you. In that sense, they are real to you. It would not sound strange to hear someone say, "No, I did not abandon you." But it would sound very strange to hear, "No, you are not feeling lonely and afraid." It simply does not make sense.

**Step 3: Express your needs.** This phrase puts some people off because they equate needs with being "needy." But needs in NVC are what arises naturally when life expresses itself. We all have needs to survive (air, water, food, shelter) and needs to thrive (touch, play, intimacy, sexual expression, creativity). We all have a need for respect and a need for our autonomy to be recognized. We also have spiritual needs, such as for peace, or wholeness, or connection with Deity. Dozens of human needs have been identified. Needs are simply life expressing itself, and they are held by all human beings. When we are in touch with our needs, we are in touch with life itself as it arises in us.

Maybe that is why we find babies so fascinating and dear. Babies are always in touch with their needs. When they are hungry, wet, or bored, they let us know immediately. And babies do not resent their needs or perceive them to be a burden on their parents. As adults we often sublimate our needs or give up on getting them met because of judgments like, "I shouldn't have this need" or "No one would give me what I need anyway."

When our needs are unmet, our fundamental humanness is denied, and when that happens, we cannot be fully human, fully happy, or fully healthy. Learning to identify our needs and how to get them met is a fundamental life skill that is part of what it means to practice spiritual speech.

Sometimes Marshall Rosenberg, in his public workshops, draws upon the work of economist Manfred Max-Neef, who presents a list of nine universal human needs: affection, creation, freedom, identity, participation, protection, recreation, subsistence, and understanding. You may find that using just these nine needs is an excellent place to start your practice of NVC; identify these needs when they arise in you.

I (Judith) once met a Rolls Royce salesman at a party. He told me that no one "needs" a Rolls Royce, and that it is his job to convince them that they do. In a few words, he summed up the basis of our consumer culture. A car is not a need but a strategy for getting a need met. What might be the need in this case? Perhaps it is for sustenance to support a family or for ease of movement when meeting commitments. The salient point is that those needs can be met by other cars, other means of transportation, other methods of getting around.

We run into trouble when we confuse strategies with needs. Most of us do this all time. We think the need is to get into a specific university or to get a certain job or to learn a certain yoga pose. But these are all strategies for getting our needs met. In the cases listed above, can you guess what the needs might be? Perhaps getting into a particular university might be a strategy for meeting a need for safety or identity. Getting a certain job might be meeting a need for community or creativity or (financial) security. And mastering a certain yoga pose might meet a need for fun or meaning or physical well-being.

Separating needs from strategies is critical in relationships. When a couple argues, it is often over strategies. For example, a couple might be arguing over where to go on vacation. One wants the beach, and the other wants the mountains. It seems like they can come to no resolution. From the point of view of NVC, this argument is about strategies. It is likely that each person has the same needs: rest and recreation. They have just chosen different strategies for meeting those needs. When the couple focuses on the needs first, the strategies often work themselves out in a mutually agreeable way.

Love is an interesting part of the needs inventory. Many people would call love a feeling, but NVC suggests that love is a need. If I have the strategy for getting love from a specific person and that person does not give it, I am stuck without getting my need for love met. But there are always many strategies for getting any particular need met, and so it is with love. I can get love from many other sources in my life. Viewing love as a need frees me up to search for another strategy to get that need met.

If we look in on the situation we visited earlier, it might go something like this: "When I see your unmade bed and the clothes on the floor of your room, I feel frustrated, because my needs for order and beauty are not met." I am being clear that the teenager's room is not the problem. Instead, by discussing the situation in this manner, I am making it clear that what is stimulating my reaction of frustration is *what is arising in me.* True, the state of the room is the stimulus for the feelings. But when I make an observation in this manner, it becomes clear that my needs are what is being discussed. The other person's actions or nonactions are not the cause of those feelings.

**Step 4: Make a request.** When I make a request, I am trying to get my needs met in that moment. Requests may seem like the easiest part of the model to understand, but actually they are more difficult to make clearly than you might think.

Requests have the following characteristics: They are made about the present, and they are doable. Requests in the NVC system are about a specific action to be done in the present. An example would be, "Are you willing to make your bed within the next five minutes?" or "Are you willing to tell me now when you might be willing to make your bed?"

It would not be a request to ask, "Would you show me that you love me?" The problem is that it is not doable. How would either person in the conversation know that the "showing love" request had been met? Showing love is not something a camera could take a picture of. A doable request might be reworded as, "Would you be willing to hug me now?" or "Would you be willing to sit on the couch now and listen to me tell you about my day for five minutes without saying anything?" These sentences are requests because not only are they referencing the present, but they ask for something that can actually be done, and in a sense measured, by the parties involved. Both people would know when the request had been met.

A request does not ask for something in the future like, "Will you wash the car tomorrow?" No one knows what they are going to do tomorrow. Instead we could ask, "Are you willing to commit now to washing the car tomorrow afternoon?" or "Are you presently willing to meet on Saturday for ten minutes to decide which health insurer we are going to use?"

The important distinction to understand when learning requests is the difference between a request and a demand. Often the only way you know when you are making a demand instead of a request is by what you do (or think of doing) when the other person says no to your request.

If you make a "perfect" request using the new phrasing you have learned and the other person still says no, and if you then respond by trying to pressure them into agreeing, you made a demand rather than a request. The sweet tone and kind face you use when asking does not make it a request. The expectation of having your request met is not in the spirit of spiritual speech.

When we have an unspoken demand, it is about power. To make a true request, we need to remain open to the outcome and open to allowing the other person to say no. (Later we discuss the next step you can take to get your needs met if your initial request is denied.)

So finally, adding a request to the scenario taking place in the teenager's room, it might sound like this: "When I see your unmade bed and the clothes on the floor of your room, I feel frustrated because my needs for order and beauty are not met. Would you spend ten minutes with me now, making the bed and picking up the clothes off the floor and hanging them in the closet?" This phrase makes a specific request; it also reveals that the request is about the needs of the speaker, which makes it more likely that the hearer will be willing to comply.

The syntax you learn in NVC is designed to help you uncover your intention—for example, the intention of connection with the other person—and remembering it in the moment. I (Ike) have found, for myself and in working with others, that using the basic sentence of NVC verbatim can be extremely valuable as you are learning this new language. We call this the "training wheels" sentence:

"When I hear _____, I feel _____, because I need _____; would you be willing to_____?"

My experience is that people who skip this step take longer to learn NVC, or they might never really

## The Four Components of Nonviolent Communication

| | | |
|---|---|---|
| 1. **Observations** | vs. | Evaluation, judgment, interpretation, diagnosis |
| Attention, awareness, acceptance | | Thinking about what happened, analysis |
| What happened, what is, facts | | Moralistic judgment, right/wrong, good/bad |
| 2. **Feelings** | vs. | Thoughts, beliefs, opinions, images |
| Emotion, body sensation | | "I feel like/that ..." |
| Feedback about our needs | | "I feel abandoned/ rejected/betrayed ..." |
| 3. **Needs** (universality) | vs. | Strategies, concrete behavior (diversity) |
| Life in action, universal qualities | | Action to meet needs |
| Language that connects to life energy | | Specific to person, time, place |
| Internal experience independent of externals | | Often cultural, habitual, conditioned |
| 4. **Requests** (for action) | vs. | Demand (coercion/power over) and vague wants |
| Response given freely, willingly | | Denial of choice: have to, should, must, can't |
| Requests as gifts of meeting needs | | Use of fear, shame, guilt, obligation, duty |
| Clear present, positive, action language | | Concept of deserving punishment or reward<br>Use of vague, abstract, future language |

integrate a "needs" consciousness. Using the training wheels sentence over and over ingrains the basic distinctions that are so important to Nonviolent Communication: distinctions between observations and judgments, between feelings and evaluations masquerading as feelings, between needs and strategies, and between requests and demands. These distinctions are embedded in the structure of the training wheels sentence, so using the sentence prompts awareness of them. Practicing the training wheels sentence is the only way I have found to establish these basic distinctions at a deep level. The sentence encourages us to focus on each of the four parts of communication—formal observations, feelings, needs, and requests. Once these are fixed in your consciousness, then you can more easily use colloquial phrasing to create the connection between yourself and others that you are seeking. When you are firm in your intention of communicating based on getting your needs met, you might even use words that sound judgmental, yet you will be able to connect with others. People often wonder why, when they are using all the "right" words, they are not getting the results they expect. Perhaps it is because they are not yet clear in their intention. When you have the clear intention of connection, the words become the strategy to accomplish this. The particular words and their syntax become secondary.

The central precept of Nonviolent Communication is to focus on connection between yourself and others, and out of that connection to fulfill your needs and the needs of others. We often believe that if we can analyze a situation clearly, we will be able to get what we want. NVC suggests that it is only when we are connected to our own needs and the needs of others that we can cooperate to meet the needs of everyone. The table on the following page identifies a number of basic feelings and needs, and might help you be more precise in expressing yourself.

## Practicing Nonviolent Communication

### *Observations*

- Write down three judgments about others and three judgments about yourself that have arisen in your mind during the past week. Now translate those judgments into observations.
- Use observation language in three interactions every day for one week. Write these down and share them with an empathy buddy: a friend who would be willing to give you empathy, and vice versa. You can be available to each other as needed, or you can speak regularly, either in person or by phone.

### *Feelings*

- For one week, at 9 a.m., 12 noon, 3 p.m., and 6 p.m., stop and note what you are feeling. Write it down.
- What feelings arise today when you believe you are right? Write them down.

## Feelings and Needs

### *Feelings*

| **Frustrated** | **Sad** | **Scared** | **Overwhelmed** |
|---|---|---|---|
| impatient | lonely, heavy | terrified | shocked |
| irritable | hurt, pained | startled | exhausted |
| annoyed | brokenhearted | nervous | helpless |
| agitated | despairing | full of dread | listless |
| disgusted | sorrowful | desperate | tired |

| **Confused** | **Peaceful** | **Affectionate** | **Happy** |
|---|---|---|---|
| hesitant | calm | warm | glad |
| distressed | content | tender | excited |
| embarrassed | satisfied | appreciative | joyful |
| suspicious | relaxed | friendly | delighted |
| puzzled | quiet, still | loving | confident |

| **Playful** | **Interested** |
|---|---|
| energetic | inspired |
| expansive | intense |
| adventurous | curious |
| mischievous | surprised |
| alive, lively | fascinated |

### *Needs*

**Well-Being**

sustenance, nourishment

safety, security, protection

health, wellness

movement, recreation

rest

balance, order

ease, flow

peace, harmony

touch

growth, learning, efficacy

wholeness

beauty

**Connection**

love, acceptance

to matter, be nurtured

intimacy, friendship

respect, consideration

equality, communion

community, belonging

to know, be known

cooperation, support

presence, awareness

understanding, clarity

honesty, trust

purpose

power, influence

inclusion, mutuality

**Expression**

celebration, play

to see, be seen

authenticity, congruence

autonomy, freedom

choice

meaning

creativity

contribution

inspiration

humor

passion

integrity

gratitude

### *Needs*

- At 9 a.m., 12 noon, 3 p.m., and 6 p.m., stop and note what you are needing at that moment. Write it down. Remember, needs are universal, and they arise in us independently of others.
- Note mentally or write down three instances in the last few days where you expressed your "needs," but they were really strategies masquerading as needs.

### *Requests*

- Think of a request you would like to make of three people. It can be the same request or three different ones. Write down these requests, refine them according to the principles of NVC, and then ask them. See what happens.
- Hear everything people say to you today as an expression of "please" or "thank you." Note how different you feel when you understand the words you hear as requests. In this case, the implied request the other is making of you is either to hear "please meet my needs" or "thank you for meeting my needs." This is true regardless of the actual words used.

# Four Communication Choices

# 3

*A new idea is first condemned as ridiculous,*
*and then dismissed as trivial, until finally*
*it becomes what everybody knows.*
—WILLIAM JAMES

SPIRITUAL SPEECH is a way of bringing the teachings of *satya* and right speech into everyday practice. Without a technique such as Nonviolent Communication, these values and ideals can remain just that. While we may value dearly the ideas of satya and right speech, how can we live them in a way that brings us home to ourselves and creates the kind of world we want to live in?

Often when we are first learning NVC, we think it is about the literal language or specific words we use. And while it is important to use the "training wheels" sentence presented in chapter 2, it is even more important to remember the primary point: Practicing NVC involves first and foremost an internal shift in awareness that allows us to use the specific language effectively. Remember, first value connecting with yourself and then allow your internal shift. Only then should you attempt to use NVC language. It is this internal shift of awareness and intention that allows speech to become a spiritual practice.

When we struggle with NVC language, it may be a sign that we have not yet made this internal shift. Use the skills you have learned in your yoga or meditation practice, or just slow down and notice what is going on inside you. Without this self-awareness, we forget that *what we say is always about ourselves*, especially about our feelings and needs, and is *never* about the other person, because whatever we say is coming out of our perception of what is. This is true even if the words we use sound like they are about or directed to the other person.

## Choice 1: Focus on Silent Self-Empathy

Starting with yourself is important, especially when you are learning. Most of us have been taught by culture and religion that focusing on ourselves is selfish and is always the worst choice. Nothing could be further from the truth. Unless and until we are aware of what we are feeling and needing, we are unlikely to relate in a direct way with others. Unless we are clear in ourselves, our words create consequences (karma) for everyone that we will probably not enjoy.

Our words live on through our relationships, and the effects of our words are passed down through the generations as "emotional DNA." Emotional DNA is just as powerful in shaping our lives as is the physical DNA we received from our ancestors. Emotional DNA creates the patterns of thinking, believing, and acting that control our lives. By using the tool of self-empathy to become aware of what is arising in us, we can begin to be clear about the patterns of speech we have inherited. We then have the choice born of awareness, and we can begin to use language in a way that heals ourselves, our children, and the world.

To practice self-empathy, sit or lie comfortably in a quiet place, and recall something someone said to you today that caused a reaction in you. You may want to write down the interchange, to slow it down in your mind. Once you have the situation in mind, distill it down to one simple sentence that the other said to you. Use observation language to start.

This means that you say to yourself, "When I remember Tom saying _____ (make an observation), I feel _____ (name the feeling that arises), because my need for _____ is not met." Make sure your observation is exactly what the other person said or did and not your judgment of it. Stay away from words such as messy, late, good, mean, and irritating; they are judgments because they imply evaluation.

Try it several times, and experiment with different

"feeling" words and different "need" words. When you find the words that are true, you will know it. Confirmation that you have hit upon something that is alive in you is often experienced as a strong physical reaction. It might be tears or a feeling of euphoria as you say the words to yourself.

Don't give up until you get some form of confirmation that is not just an intellectual awareness. This energetic shift is the manifestation that you have connected with your deepest self. You have given yourself empathy for what is alive in you. Life is now serving life. There is something healing about naming what is going on inside you.

Finally, another way you will know that you have connected with yourself is that you will notice a curiosity about the other person, about what might have been going on with them when the communication happened, or what might be going on with them now. Our advice is to persevere with silent self-empathy until this curiosity arises in you. It may take more than one session to arrive at this place of curiosity.

If you try to force yourself to be interested in what is alive in the other person before you are ready, thoughts may arise like, "I don't really care what that so-and-so is feeling or needing right now." If that happens, continue with your process of self-empathy until you can think of the other with an open heart and you feel compassion, or at least curiosity, arising in yourself for the other.

## Choice 2: Focus on Self-Expression

The second communication choice is self-expression. This means that you state aloud to the other person what is going on with you. Again, use the training wheels sentence while you are learning: "When I heard you close the door with more force than I like, I felt irritated, because my need for respect and peace was not met." (Note the use of observation language: "with more force than I like" instead of "slammed." "Slammed" conveys a judgment that the other person can definitely argue with you about.) Do not fail to follow this self-expression with a clear, doable request. If you stop with the first sentence, the other person may very well begin to argue with you and say things like, "I didn't slam the door" or "you always say that" or "I can never do anything right for you, can I?" Without a doable request, people often hear the expression of observations, feelings, and needs as criticism. (You will follow your self-expression with an immediate request, detailed below.)

The whole interchange would then be: "When I heard you close the door with more force than I like, I felt irritated, because my need for respect and peace was not met. Would you tell me ...". Here is where you make your request, which is detailed under the fourth communication choice. Make sure the whole interchange uses no more than thirty words. Using more words is likely to result in disconnection.

Remember, even if you make a request using "perfect" NVC language, the person may still hear criticism and judgment. If so, give yourself self-empathy again and try once more. Remember, NVC is a practice like yoga and meditation and therefore requires lots of repetition. Your intention is not to get it right but to connect with yourself and with the person in front of you. It is this connection that holds the potential for changing the world.

### Choice 3: Focus on Giving Empathy

The third choice, either to begin or to continue your communication process, is to focus on giving the other person empathy. This can either be silent empathy in your own heart or empathy spoken out loud. When I (Judith) first learned about silent empathy, I was not impressed. I thought, How can what I think make any difference unless I actually tell the other person what I'm thinking?

Then I tried using silent empathy and was astounded by what happened. I learned that when I use silent empathy with the other person, a change happens. *But that change occurs in me.* This is so because, in order to empathize silently with the other person, I have to empathize with myself first. In the beginning of my practice of Nonviolent Communication, silent self-empathy could take minutes, hours, or days. Now, with practice, I can sometimes feel the shift that comes with self-empathy in a matter of seconds, and then I can choose to give empathy to the other almost immediately. I actually now experience self-empathy and empathy for the other as virtually the same process, like a continuum.

Silent empathy for the other person also causes a change in my expression and body language that the other person picks up. This shift is sometimes palpable between us, and invariably when I shift, the other person senses it and shifts as well. Ike and I are both continually amazed and pleased by how powerful it is to give the other person silent empathy.

To give silent empathy is to intuit or guess what the other person might be feeling or needing in the moment. Be sure to start with observation language. Your inner dialogue might go something like this: "When I heard her say _____, I am guessing that she was feeling _____ and needing _____." It does not matter if you are correct about what is "true" for her. Rather, it is the process of considering the other person after having empathized with your own needs that fuels the shift. When you make this shift to compassion, you will have a greater potential to actually say what you want to say.

The other empathic choice is to give empathy to the other person out loud. Remember, it is not about being "right" with your guesses; it is about honoring the intention of connecting with the other. This intention reflects the spirit of *satya*, which is not just telling the truth but has inherent in it the desire to better the world. The best way to learn empathic guessing is to do it. Give yourself silent empathy all day long when judgments arise, and then try it with others. And watch the magic happen! (See the exercises at the end of the chapter for practice in offering empathic guessing.)

One important distinction to keep in mind when you are choosing empathy is the difference between empathy and sympathy. Empathy is focused on the other, on their feelings and needs. Sympathy is listening to the other and then shifting the emphasis to yourself as a way to connect—for example, "I know just how you feel; my dog died last March." While offering sympathy is often well-intentioned, it takes the focus of the communication from the other person and back to yourself. As a practice, notice when you use sympathy instead of using an empathetic guess.

One experience of giving empathy particularly stands out for me (Ike). In January 2002, in the aftermath of the attacks of September 11 and the kidnapping of *Wall Street Journal* reporter Daniel Pearl, NVC trainer John Kinyon and I offered three days of NVC conflict resolution training in the Shamsatu refugee camp, near Peshawar, Pakistan.

Our travels in Pakistan took us northwest, toward the Afghan border, near the Khyber Pass. We had to gain access to the camps from the head of security for all refugee camps for the 1.1 million Afghan refugees, Lt. Col. Abdula Hafeez. We answered his skeptical questions for nearly ten minutes as we tried to "sell" him on the idea of our offering a training, but he remained understandably reluctant to grant us permission. His shift from skepticism to willingness did not occur until we spent the next ten minutes guessing what he was feeling and needing. Then, in one of the fastest shifts I have ever seen, he leaned forward on his desk and wrote out a pass to the camp, complete with two security officers detailed to us, instructions to the camp administrator that he was to accompany us at all times, and a message to be sent ahead to the camp to invite all the elders to meet with us.

We offered the training session for the leaders of the various tribes represented in the camp, which held 1,100 families who had fled the many years of violence in Afghanistan. We had planned to teach the principles of NVC from day one, but there was so much pain being expressed that we could not move past giving empathy for the first two days. These people had lived in the so-called "temporary" camps for years; they had been promised so much by so many, and much of it had never materialized. They were no longer living in their country, their children did not have many of the things we take for granted, and their future was unsettled, to say the least.

Instead of spending our time teaching, as we had planned, we found ourselves responding to the immediate pain and anguish in front of us, which was directly stimulated by us being American. This anguish was created in part by what the United States had done in Afghanistan—by leaving as soon as the Soviets had withdrawn and not following through with promises of support. All the pain and suffering of nearly twenty-five years of turmoil and war boiled over in our interaction with these men.

With each cycle of empathy, we could see plainly the wonder of empathic connection. When our guesses about their feelings and needs turned out to be true for them, the speakers would fall silent, their eyes would lower, and the other twenty-five or so men sitting on the floor around the room would murmur together in assent. The muscles around the speaker's eyes would relax, his jaw would soften, and a glistening of tears would appear in his eyes. This would be followed by ten or twenty seconds of reflective silence without eye contact. We felt the empathic connection as a palpable entity. We went through tens of these cycles in the first two days alone.

We learned once again that needs are universal and are part of all human beings, even when those needs are translated from English to Urdu to Pastho and then at times into Uzbek, Tajik, Turkmen, and or Parsi, via ad hoc translations. On the surface, our seeming differences of dress, life experiences, culture, education, and resources separated us, and yet, with the sharing of our feelings and needs, I saw beyond the differences to how we are all truly the same. These were men, just like me, who wanted to contribute to the well-being of their families and others, and who were distressed because they needed order and stability. They wanted education for their children. They wanted to trust that commitments when made would be kept. They were longing for hope, hope for a world where, as one man put it, doctors would work as doctors, and engineers as engineers, and shopkeepers as shopkeepers, referring to so many who were instead working at manual labor.

At the beginning of the last day, a Friday, the Islamic holy day, one of the men invited us to join him in prayer at the mosque that afternoon. Immediately another man objected, saying that we could not go to the mosque because we were not Muslim. We had been looking for a "real" conflict to use as an example in the group, and John Kinyon seized on this opportunity. I did have some concern that our role play was about something as real and sensitive as nonbelievers at Islamic prayer services, but we decided to go ahead, since this was actually what had arisen in the group.

The invitation to the mosque became our example of conflict. With some coaching, the needs were identified. Those who wanted us to join them in prayer at the mosque needed understanding, connection, and education. Those who objected needed respect for that which helped them make sense out of their world—their religion. Each side reflected back those needs to the other side. Then John asked his question: "Is there anyone here who does not share these needs?"

An excited murmur of insight and awareness filled the room. Yes, of course, seemed to be the response, we see how we all share these needs, and we can respect them in ourselves and others.

The brainstorming for an actual strategy to meet the needs took only moments. In retrospect, our solution seemed simple, as they often do when each person feels heard. We all agreed that the Westerners in the room who had not been raised in Islam would receive a fifteen- or twenty-minute explanation of the ceremony, and that they would sit outside the doors of the mosque and observe from there. Finally, they would be welcomed into the mosque at the completion of Friday afternoon prayers. We had solved our "conflict" in a way that connected us to them, them to us, and all of us to each other. John and I were profoundly moved by the experience, one that still gives me hope for how the world can be.

At the end of the last session, one of the elders said to us, referring to the NVC training, "If we could do this, we would have no more war."

## Choice 4: Focus on Other: Request

Once you have practiced self-expression and empathy for the other, it is time—and quickly—to make a request. There are two types of requests. The first is an *action request,* which is simply to ask for the action you would like the other person to take. While this sounds easy, we have often found it to be difficult.

After 9/11, Ike and I (Judith) wanted to write a letter to the president expressing our feelings and needs and making requests about the course we wanted him to take. We found that we could very easily write what we didn't want him to do, but it took several days for us to come up with and write what we did want him to do. We wrote that we wanted him to respond using a model of justice and police enforcement rather than a military model.

While Ike was applying NVC in legal mediations, I attempted to apply NVC as I taught my yoga classes. I liked how using NVC helped me make clear requests of my students. In a way, every time I say to my yoga class "Utthita Trikonasana," I am making a request. But I cannot "make" the student do the pose; I can really only ask. So the question is, how will I ask? Will I ask in a way that will be more likely to have my request granted? Or will I ask in a way that is perceived as a demand? When I make a demand, I create a distance between the student and me. If instead I make a true request, I am remaining open not only in my choice of words but also to how they are received. When I make a request instead of a demand, I speak from a deep respect for the student and for myself. I predict that requesting with awareness, respect, and openness will create connection between the student and me. This is what I want: connection and compassion between human beings. I can begin to create this connection when I am clear about whether I am demanding or requesting.

Whether I am making a request or a demand is not determined by the way my sentence sounds. Instead, I know the difference by how I feel inside my body if the request or demand is refused. If it was a request, I will just ask again in another way and attempt to find out what might be keeping the student from meeting my request. If my request was really a demand, then I will react in my body, often with feelings that come from thinking that the student should do what I am asking.

As a yoga teacher, before I studied NVC, I occasionally felt irritated when a student in class did not respond to my demand, but I never understood why I felt that way. I may ask a student to attempt Urdhva Mukha Vrksasana (Handstand), and she may be hesitant. Am I demanding or requesting? How can I request in a way that will make it delicious for the student to choose Handstand?

If I make a true request, then this delicious choice is a real possibility. With my intention, I have opened the world by reminding myself and the student to hold as precious the understanding that we are all at choice. This is a deeply rewarding way to communicate, in part because it so accurately reflects the way the world actually is. By asking, "Are you willing to . . . ," I make it clear that I only want people to do what they are willing to do. On the one hand, if they act on my request from a place of obligation, even if they do what I want, we will both "pay," and it won't be satisfying for either of us. On the other hand, if the other person responds to my request with willingness, we are connecting to meet each other's needs. The fulfilling of the request becomes almost a form of service in the spiritual sense of the word. The second type of request is a *process request*. This type of request is asking the other person one of two questions: Would you tell me what you just heard me say? Or, how do you feel hearing what I just said?

We have found both of these requests to be very useful. The first, "Would you tell me what you just heard me say," is an attempt to make sure that the message you sent with your observations, feelings, and needs was the message that was actually received. This process can sometimes be like the children's game Whisper, where each child in a circle of children whispers a phrase to the next, and so on to the last child, who says it out loud. The game is funny because the phrase reported by the last person is never even close to what the first child whispered.

It happens with adult communication too. You may think that you're being very clear, but what the other person hears may be somehow not what you said or intended. Check this out with a friend or with your empathy buddy. Try reflecting what you hear or asking for what you said until the sender of the message is satisfied that they have been heard correctly.

By asking the person to tell you what they heard, you are meeting your needs for clarity and connection. It is important that the other person understands that this is not a test of their abilities. You can make that clear by listening to what they say and responding with some form of "thank you," such as, "Thank you for your willingness to tell me what you heard." We suggest that you thank them, regardless of what the other person says back to you. They have done what you asked, which was to tell you what they heard. If they heard something different than what you wanted to say, now you know that, and you can try again to be heard as you would like. If you are satisfied that they understood what you were saying, then proceed with the communication by making the request again or by making another request.

If you are not satisfied that the person got what you said, then try again. Break down your communication into smaller bites. One way to do this might be to say, "I would like you to hear something different, so let me say it this way." Give them a smaller piece of what is true for you, using fewer words, if possible. Then ask them again to tell you what they heard. If they react negatively to this, start over with self-empathy and empathy for the other. Maybe they are not able to reflect back what you said because they are still in need of empathy. When you are satisfied that you have been heard, you may want to proceed further.

The second process request, "How do you feel hearing what I just said," is an attempt, in a shorthand way, to assess whether the listener's needs are being met or not. You may have just said something that has a great deal of meaning for the other. She may be overwhelmed or confused by what you just said. The communication most likely will not proceed as you want if the other person feels irritated, for instance, by what you are saying, and you don't realize it. Also, by asking the other to tell you what is alive in her, what she is feeling, you are helping her to connect with her own inner states. You are stimulating self-awareness in the other. And you are using your words to connect you both to the present moment. This is the essence of spiritual speech.

## Practicing Nonviolent Communication

### *Practicing self-empathy*

- Find a quiet place, and remember an interaction of the past week that you did not enjoy. Now write down a self-empathy phrase about it. Begin with the observation, then write your feelings, and guess your needs that were not met by what was said or done. If you have difficulty guessing what you were feeling or needing, set the paper aside and revisit it tomorrow or the next day. Keep at it until you feel the internal shift we get from receiving empathy, even from ourselves.
- The next time someone stimulates a reaction in you, say, "Excuse me for five minutes." Then go into another room, and give yourself empathy until you feel curious about what is going on with the other

## Communication Choices

| *Where Is My Focus?* | *Silent Communication* | *Spoken Communication* |
|---|---|---|
| On myself | Choice 1.<br>Self-Empathy:<br>Naming to myself what I am observing, feeling, needing, requesting | Choice 2.<br>Self-Expression:<br>Saying how I am feeling and requesting what I would like without blame, criticism, or demand |
| On the other person | Choice 3.<br>Silent Empathy:<br>Guessing what the other is observing, feeling, needing, requesting | Choice 3.<br>Giving Empathy:<br>Guessing how another is feeling and what they might be requesting without blame, criticism, or demand |
| On the other person | | Choice 4.<br>Making a Request:<br>Make an action request or a process request, asking for feedback. |

## The Two Types of Requests

| | |
|---|---|
| Action requests: | A strategy to meet everyone's needs:<br>"Would you be willing to ...?" |
| Process requests: | For reflection:<br>"Would you tell me what you heard me say?"<br><br>For response:<br>"How do you feel hearing what I say?" |

person. Then return to conversation. (If you do not feel curious, that is a sign you need more self-empathy. Continue giving yourself empathy about your feelings and needs until you begin to care about the other person in the situation.)

### *Practicing self-expression*

- Tell someone close to you, perhaps your empathy buddy, that you are experimenting with a new way of communicating. Then ask them to listen as you say something with your old style of communicating and then with your newly learned NVC way of expressing. Remember the sentence, "When I hear you say that, I feel _____, because my need for _____ is not met. Would you be willing to _____?" Try this process at least once each day until it becomes more familiar and less awkward.
- Use self-expression when you call a technical help line or customer service number. Follow the "training wheels" sentence in chapter 2, and listen to how effective it is in this context. I (Judith) used my calls to customer service lines when I was learning NVC to practice. The first time I did it, I felt a little silly, but not only did I get excellent service, the representative called me back in ten minutes with a solution to my problem that moments before she said would take a week. Begin with empathy for the other. One way to start is: "Hello, I can imagine that you are

really busy today, but I really want you to hear how important this is to me."

### *Giving empathy*

- The next time you are waiting in line at the airport or in a store and your turn comes up, open the conversation by giving empathy to the person behind the counter. Say something like, "Are you feeling overwhelmed by the number of customers?" or "It looks like you are really busy today and have lots of unhappy customers." Notice how the person responds.
- Today, when someone complains to you about the government, the weather, or his favorite sports team, instead of joining in, respond with empathy. Say something like, "So when you say that, are you wanting me to hear how irritated you are by what _____ (name the person) did about that issue?" Continue to give empathy until the person begins to shift and a feeling of connection occurs. It may take several rounds of empathy. Or it may take several conversations until they feel heard. You might use something like this as well: "It sounds like her actions did not meet your needs for integrity and compassion." Observe how the other person begins to change and how much more connected you feel.

### *Making a request*

- Whenever you want something from someone today, say, "Are you willing to . . ." when you ask for it. Be sure to be specific about what you are asking her to do. For example, "Are you willing to make your bed and hang up your clothes by 6 p.m., when our guests are arriving?"

- The next time you are in a meeting, observe how people do not make clear requests of others. They often say things like, "Yes, let's do that" or "That sounds like a great idea," but they do not request a specific action from specific people at a specific time.

# 4 Listening to Ourselves and Others

*Human beings are perhaps never more frightening than when they are convinced beyond doubt that they are right.*

—LAURENS VAN DER POST

IN ONE OF my early seminars with Marshall Rosenberg, he said something that stimulated anger in me (Judith). His words were: "Never do anything that doesn't give you the joy of a three-year-old feeding a hungry duck." While I liked the vividness of this image, my response was swift and emotional. I said to myself, "Well then, I wouldn't do half my life. We have to do things we don't want to do, or life would fall apart."

Immediately I began to observe my reaction to his words and to give myself empathy for the words that had bubbled up in response to his. But for several years I found that I could not accept what he had said. I had beliefs or judgments about it, like, "Doing only what you want to do is indulgent and selfish." I did not enjoy the language I was using toward myself; I did not enjoy the judgments I was having about myself for having those judgments. I was caught in a hall of mirrors; I was judging myself for judging myself.

This circle of judgment is a common process for many people. The way we listen to our self-dialogue can be one of compassion or one of judgment, but whichever we choose, it is a powerfully life-shaping process. My (internal) words reflect my thoughts, and my thoughts reflect my beliefs, and these beliefs, especially the unconscious ones, run my life. The practice of *satya* and right speech begins at home, when I give myself empathy for my beliefs. These days my inner dialogue is shaped by NVC. It clearly hasn't always been so.

When I was growing up, I "heard" many messages from my family, culture, and church that told me to deny my needs. I am not saying those were the lessons that were taught, but they were the lessons I heard. I was taught that to do so was right and unselfish and in service to God. So I learned to get my needs met by the strategy of not really asking for what I needed. In fact, I tried specifically to not reveal what I needed, in order to avoid being judged as "needy" or demanding. I do not believe I am alone in this; women especially seem to be raised as I was: trained to look after everyone else's needs and to deny the existence of their own. "I live to serve" was my motto. Marshall Rosenberg addresses this issue when he states provocatively but kindly, "Women have no needs." Of course, he is trying to draw our attention to this issue by making such a ridiculous statement. Unfortunately, the statement was all too true for me. Or so it seemed.

Remember, to acknowledge our needs is not to be demanding. All human needs are the expression of life's energy flowing through us. Needs are the very thing that connect us to life itself. When we become aware of our needs and the needs of others and long to meet those needs, we are honoring the sacredness of life.

As I have learned, the problem with living in a way that denies my needs is that it sets the stage for me to do violence to myself. That violence is taken out on me by me, but it could just as well be taken out on another. If I act from violence to myself or others, I am not contributing to the peaceful world I want to create. I am not living from my highest values. I am not living the spirit of satya or right speech.

If I do something for you because I should, or because it is "spiritual" to act that way, or because it makes me a "good person," a residue will be left. This residue is often resentment, and resentment poisons relationships and diminishes life. Paradoxically, I will end up taking it out on you, because in a twisted way I blame you for me not getting my needs met.

In order to learn more about my own needs, I began to check in with myself several times a day to see what I happened to be needing at that moment. I would then give myself empathy. And I found out something interesting. I always could guess what I was feeling, but I had a hard time guessing what I was needing. Ike, on the other hand, always knew what he was needing but did not seem to know what he was feeling. He later reported that at that period of his life he had only two feelings: OK and angry.

I began to observe that I frequently did things not because they met my needs but because I was afraid of the judgment that I predicted would come from the other person if I said no. For example, Ike would ask me to go to the movies, and even if I didn't want to go, I would say yes. Then, when we went to the movie, I would complain about it and somehow make it hard for us to enjoy ourselves. Or I would say no to going to the movie, then feel guilty about saying no, and be "too nice" to him for the next couple of days. I bounced between resentment and being overly nice; I thought that was what a marriage relationship was.

## The Duck Index

Because of my personal lack of awareness about my needs, I realized I needed a specific strategy to help me learn and practice. So I created what I call the "duck index." I love the image of a squealing, delighted little child running and throwing pieces of stale bread for a flock of ducks by a lake. I smile every time I think of it.

My duck index has a scale of 1 to 10. I decided I would not to do anything unless it was at least a 6 on my index, and then I would see what happened. As I used the duck index, I learned first to get in touch with my needs and then to trust that understanding. The next time Ike asked me to a movie I didn't want to see, I checked in with myself and responded with, "That's a 3 on my duck index." But that was not the end of the matter. The next thing I said was, "But seduce me with your needs."

In other words, just because someone asks us to do something we don't want to do, something that is not high on our duck index, doesn't mean the negotiation is closed. We could be open to shifting. Shifting is not at all the same as giving in. Just saying yes to all requests is giving in. To shift is to hear the needs of the other and to feel that to meet them would also meet your needs.

So when I said, "Seduce me with your needs," I was acknowledging this reality. I was telling Ike that I was open to shifting so that meeting his needs would also meet mine. Marshall Rosenberg states, "My needs first and foremost, but never my needs at the expense of your needs." Shifting is the process of attempting to meet both my needs and the needs of the other person.

Remember two things about the distinction between strategies and needs. Strategies are ways of getting needs met, and needs are never in conflict; only strategies are in conflict. At any given time, there are always many strategies that can meet any particular need.

When we cling to a specific strategy as the only way to meet a need, we suffer if that strategy does not bear fruit.

In the preceding example, the movie was not a need; it was a strategy for getting a need met. When I asked Ike what needs he was attempting to meet by suggesting we go to the movie, he said his needs were fun, entertainment, and companionship. When I heard those needs, I immediately shifted from a 3 to a 5 on my duck index. I felt an actual shift in my body. After a couple more rounds of sharing needs and empathy, I was still at a 5 and so did not "force" myself to go. Then we brainstormed about other ways we might both get our needs met, and we ended up satisfied. The whole thing took ten minutes, and we ended the evening still in connection with one another.

So what happens when I agree to do something because it is an 8 on my duck index, but when the time comes to follow through, it might have gone down to a 4. This happens to all of us occasionally. On Monday the idea of going to my friend's party on Friday night is an 8, but after a long week, when Friday night arrives, and it's raining, and I'm tired, going to the party seems like a 4. How do I meet my need for rest and my friend's need for companionship at the same time?

First and always, give yourself empathy for the lack of enthusiasm you are feeling right now about following through with the plan. In other words, guess specifically what is alive in you now. When that process feels complete, and you are connected fully with your needs, then connect now with the needs you were trying to meet then, when you said yes. Again give yourself empathy. When that is complete, give silent empathy to your friend. What needs is she attempting to meet by inviting you to the party?

The last step is to call your friend and express your needs. Tell her what is true for you. It might go something like this: "On Monday, when I said I would come to the party, I was excited. But now I have a great need for rest. How do you feel hearing that?" When she tells you her feelings, give her empathy for whatever you guess is up for her—perhaps hurt or disappointment. Once you have made empathic connection with her, ask, "Would you be willing to brainstorm for five minutes other strategies we can use to meet both your need for companionship (assuming that is the need) and my need for rest?"

Here is a crucial point: be open to any outcome. A number of things could happen. She could be totally fine with you not coming, or you could shift and decide to go after talking to her and extrapolating her needs, or you could both decide to get together tomorrow, or you could agree that you would take a nap and come to the party later. The point is that, through this process, you would both get your needs met.

It may sound like all this would take some time, and it does. But how much time would it take to not go through this process of connection? How much time and suffering would disconnection with your needs and your friend's needs cost in the long run?

Many people are reluctant to ask for their needs to be met because they believe their needs are a burden to others. This way of thinking has two consequences. First, you don't allow others the gift of giving you what you need. Think of a baby. Babies do not hesitate to ask for their needs to be met, and they tend to do so strongly and immediately. But as adults, we often hide our needs, because we feel they are not worthy of being met. Even if my needs are not a gift to you, I like how I behave when I choose to think they are.

It might be useful here to remember the distinction between requesting and demanding. Making a demand for your needs to be met, or a demand for anything, is to not include the other in the process. Demanding implies that there are consequences, presumably negative consequences, for the other person if they do not do as you ask. Requesting means you are open to the outcome.

## Please and Thank You

Another way to listen in a new way to your inner voice is to hear whatever anyone says to you as a request. Specifically, translate everything anyone says to you as either a "please" or a "thank you." This is one of my (Judith's) favorite techniques.

Here's how to do it. One day I stopped my car at a

red light and was a little bit too far into the crosswalk. A man who was crossing yelled at me, calling me a stupid driver. I would usually take this sort of thing to heart and feel terrible about my actions. My inner dialogue would be filled with lots of judgments about myself. Other people might do the opposite, thinking how stupid or rude the man was being.

On that day, I decided to try hearing what he said as a request, in particular as a "please," a technique I had just learned. So I said to myself, What if he said it this way: "Please hear how afraid I was that you might have hit me and injured me." When I translated "stupid driver" into "please hear my fear," I felt compassion arise in me for him and for myself. I really liked how I felt about the situation then; I was just a human being, as was he, doing the best we could. I felt neither angry at him nor angry at myself. It was a red-letter day.

Another example is a conversation I had with my teenage daughter. She asked me to pick her up after school, adding, "And Mom, please don't act like a dork." I could have chosen to respond with hurt or by correcting her for being "rude," but instead I chose to hear the following: "Mom, please hear how tender I am around my friends. I am so afraid they will reject me, and I don't want to give them any ammunition to do that. Please help me by not standing out and attracting any attention." Whether or not this statement was what she was feeling and needing, I liked how I shifted to a more compassionate state when I decided to hear it that way. William James said, "The greatest weapon we have to combat stress is the ability to choose our thoughts." When we choose to hear the other's statement as "please hear my pain," we have the choice to act in a way that will connect us with them. This ability to choose to react to those around us with awareness is what makes speech a spiritual practice.

"Thank you" is another thing people say to us all day long. When they say, "That was a great yoga class" or "I really enjoyed the meal; it was good," they are saying "thank you." When I hear that I was good or did something good, I feel vaguely uneasy. I know that if I am good, I can also be bad. Once I am on the good–bad or right–wrong continuum, I can go either way. I may not be able to do it again or in the right way, and I feel nervous about that.

But now, instead of hearing their statement as being about me, I hear it as being about them. I translate what they are saying into a request: "Please hear how much your class (or meal) met my needs." When I translate their statements into "thank you for meeting my needs," I am reinforcing the understanding that I am not the source of another's happiness. The fact that I met their needs was about their needs getting met, not about me being good or right. Hearing their statement as a request for me to understand that needs were met makes it simpler and cleaner. I am only part of the dance of communication then, and I like being partners with others in that way.

## Practicing Nonviolent Communication

### *Duck index*

- Tell your family or roommates about the duck index, and begin to practice it over small things, like what you would like for dinner or what time you want to go shopping with them. Celebrate your newfound clarity.
- The next time someone asks a favor of you that is low on your duck index, say, "That's not high on my duck index, but seduce me with your needs." Be open to shifting, so that it might become something you want to do. Only say yes if you have shifted.

### *Please and thank you*

- Notice today how often someone says "thank you" to you. After one of those times, ask the person to tell you exactly what you said or did that caused them to say "thank you."
- Think of a time in the last couple of days when you said something in irritation to someone close to you, such as, "Why are you always late?" Translate your statement of irritation into a "please" statement. If possible, go back to the other person and say, "What I really meant to say the other day was 'Please hear how afraid I felt when you did not come home at the time we agreed and did not call me to say you were OK.' I was upset because I care about you and your well-being, and I wanted you to know that." Note their response.

# 5 What We Say Matters

*People heal by having an authentic connection with an authentic human being.*
—Martin Buber

Many years ago, I (Judith) had a conversation with Usharbudh Arya (now Swami Veda), a practitioner of yoga since childhood and a scholar of Sanskrit and the ancient texts of India. My question was, "Which is more important, the practice of *ahimsa,* nonharming, or the practice of *satya,* truth?" (Both are part of *yama,* or the first limb of the traditional yoga of Patanjali.) I wanted to know how to choose between these yamas in my practice. Should I tell someone the truth that might hurt them, or tell them something "kind" instead, to avoid harming them?

Swamiji's answer surprised me. He said, "Something cannot be true and unkind at the same time." This answer still echoes in my ears as I attempt to use the techniques of Nonviolent Communication to express my desire to practice satya and right speech. Both Ike and I have talked about the seeming conflict between truth and nonharming, and we have clarified for ourselves two values for guiding our speech that we feel reflect Swami Veda's wisdom.

First, we hold is that speech is a *power* that we can choose to use for fostering connection between and among people. In order to do that, however, we must first connect with ourselves. This ability to turn inward and be in connection with self in a truthful way lies at the heart of spiritual speech. Without self awareness, it is likely that you will not speak with the words you want.

Second, we believe that "truth" is what is alive in me at this very moment. That is my truth. I can only speak from what is alive in me right now. Not only is this all I can do, but it is the best way to bring my connection with others to life. When I speak from what is alive in me right now, I am present with myself. When I speak from that space, I model and encourage others to do the same.

This practice will change the world. It will change your life, and it will affect others in a profound and distinct way. When you create an atmosphere of trust and connection with your words, there is little that cannot get worked out between people. What greater gift can we give the world than our own true selves?

I once heard Marshall Rosenberg state in a seminar

what it means to speak in a "spiritual" way: "It respects the conditions in which all members of the world community can live in dignity and freedom, without destroying each other's chances of livelihood, society, or culture." This is a practical expression of spiritual speech, and it expresses values that Ike and I both hold dear. *What we say matters,* not only because it changes the immediate relationship we are in right now, but also because it shapes the future by leaving a legacy of clarity and connection among human beings.

## Dealing with Anger

The experience of anger and its expression in speech is a daily experience for most of us. One day I decided to count the number of times I felt frustration, irritation, or anger. I bought a small handheld counter and counted every little ripple that arose. The number at the end of the day was astounding to me: sixty-seven.

Perhaps that is not a typical number, but with road rage and violence all around us, perhaps it is. As Marshall Rosenberg points out, and as we have experienced in our own lives, anger, along with shame, guilt, and depression, are a special class of feelings that arise out of judging how the world should be.

With feelings like joy, connection, or disappointment, there is nothing hidden underneath the feeling. But if you inquire further of yourself, you will find other feelings lurking underneath anger. These hidden feelings are usually one or a combination of hurt, fear, or frustration.

This was hard for us to hear. Ike reports that in the beginning of his study of NVC, the only two feelings he could really identify were OK and angry. I (Judith) remember the first time I learned from a meditation teacher about the arising of anger. The practice she was giving was to be present with what was arising within us as we sat on the cushion. That was it, no other technique. Furthermore, she suggested that beginning meditation students typically spend most of the first few years on the meditation cushion realizing how angry they are.

Believe it or not, this profound teaching stimulated irritation in me. (How ironic.) Then I began a consistent meditation practice and realized how right she was. What I usually felt was not a full-blown fury but rather the "little anger" of mild frustration, of irritation, of wishing it were different, whatever "it" was—wishing my back didn't hurt, wishing the neighbor would stop mowing her lawn at 6:30 a.m. when I was trying to meditate, wishing I was not feeling irritated at the neighbor. This mental process of irritation (or even anger) can continue and echo through the mind almost forever, or so it would seem.

Take a quiet moment and remember a time recently when you felt angry. Reflect now on how you felt then. As you consider it, give yourself empathy by guessing now what was alive in you in that moment of anger. It's very likely you will discover that at its root it was hurt, frustration, or fear. One of these three emotions is probably a more accurate expression of what you were feeling underneath your anger at the time.

When you discover what was alive in you, you will shift. This shift, as mentioned before, will be not only a shift in perception but also a shift in bodily sensation. For me this shift is a verification that I have discovered my truth.

One day I decided to test this theory. The next time I remembered something that day that had stimulated anger in me, I connected with myself using the process of self-empathy. I noticed immediately that I was in my head, telling myself over and over, "How could he say that to me? Who does he think he is?"

Then I purposely focused on the sensations in my belly and tried to guess what feeling might really be alive in me. Suddenly I got it; I wasn't angry really; I was hurt when I recalled what the other person had said. When I began to think again about what the other had said, I immediately moved into my thoughts, and I felt anger again. Down to the belly and into feeling, up to the head and lost in thoughts and judgment: I did this dance four or five times, a smile slowly growing across my face. I finally understood. Anger was stimulated by my thoughts and judgments about the situation and was a strategy for hiding my feeling of hurt. My anger was helping me protect myself from hurt. I was building a wall of protection, using anger as my tool.

One day Ike and I entered a large hall for a seminar. I noticed a man across the room who I labeled "the angry man." When the moderator asked us to take a seat away from the person we had come with, I made a beeline to a seat as far as I could get from the man I had labeled. Of course, he came and sat by me, and we ended up being partners for a number of exercises. Ironically, if we are living our own anger, we tend to attract it in others. Not only that, but if we have unresolved anger, we tend to scan the environment looking for it in others. We will always find it, just as I did in the seminar.

When was the last time your anger reached another person's heart? Anger is not effective in connecting us with ourselves or with others. It is not an effective tool for communicating with those we care about.

The next time you find yourself angry with someone, take some time to give yourself empathy until you recognize what you are telling yourself that is causing you to feel angry. Then empathize with the need you are seeking to meet by what you're saying to yourself. Chances are you will be much happier with what you say to the other person if you take care of yourself first.

## Righteous Anger and Social Change

Most of us are familiar with the term "righteous anger." It is used to mean the anger that has a "good" or socially acceptable cause. Actually, all anger has a righteous quality. You cannot be angry unless you believe you are right. You would never say, "I am so mad at you, and I am completely wrong." Feeling that you are right always fuels anger. And anger disconnects us from ourselves and from others. Anger is a wall that keeps us dead to what is really going on within us.

A Buddhist story addresses the issue of righteous anger. One day a monk found an abandoned rowboat by the shore of the lake near his monastery. After trying unsuccessfully to find the owner of the rowboat, he spent his free time restoring it. The day finally came to launch the beautiful new boat. It was a little misty on the lake, but he settled into the boat and rowed out onto the water. Suddenly out of the mist came another rowboat, and it plowed into his new boat and damaged its prow. The monk got angry and thought, "Who would be so careless as to run into me and damage my boat?" I am guessing that this anger was fueled by the thought that he was right and had been wronged by the person in the other boat.

As the other boat came closer, it turned out to be empty; it had just drifted into his boat. With that, the monk's anger melted away. There was no one to blame. When we can recognize anger for what it is, we understand our needs and the needs of others, and we are more likely to choose words that reflect that understanding. *Everything is an empty rowboat.*

While we may feel a commitment to social change,

fueling it with anger disconnects us from the heart of compassion. Anger prevents us from practicing ahimsa in its deepest form. When you want to change some circumstance, first use self-empathy to connect yourself to your needs, and then act in a way that furthers the social change you value.

## Enemy Images

One of the surest ways to disconnect from ourselves and temporarily forget the values of satya and right speech is to project enemy images onto other people or even onto ourselves. This projection can be onto our family, neighbors, or political figures we have never met. When we have enemy images, we make a moralistic judgment about ourselves or others, believing that they or we are evil.

When you are in conflict with someone and you tell yourself negative judgments about them, these "enemy images" leak out and color the interaction. Whatever I think of you will influence my body language, my expression, and my words. And you will sense these judgments, even if I don't express them with words. Connection will be difficult, if not impossible.

Carrying enemy images into a meeting or conversation almost guarantees that you will not get your needs met. If you are going into a meeting or conversation with someone for whom you have enemy images, do self-empathy and then silent empathy for the other until your feelings have shifted. This may take days or even weeks.

You may also choose to seek the help of an experienced NVC trainer to help you with this issue, if you are in a lot of pain. You may even want to write out your goals—of ahimsa and connection, for example—on a piece of paper and have that in front of you while you talk with the other person. It will help you to stay focused on your values throughout the meeting.

Make no mistake: Acknowledging our enemy images, choosing to transform them by finding the need behind the judgment, and getting help to do this is not work for the fainthearted. Society supports the habits of thinking and talking using enemy images. But if we are committed to self-transformation and the transformation of the world, we will learn to speak from a place without enemy images.

Let's be clear: Transforming enemy images does not mean we give up passion for our values or belief in our cause. It does mean that we do not put the other person or ourselves in a box labeled "evil, wrong, or bad" and then try to interact with them. We can certainly disagree with others' actions and choices, even to the point of believing that they should be incarcerated to protect those around them. But the practice of nonharming is to see the other person as a human being who is suffering, as we all are, and to think, act, and speak from compassion. NVC is a powerful tool for helping us to do exactly that.

## The Joy of Interrupting

Marshal Rosenberg reports that, in some countries in the world, no one will interrupt you, even in an unproductive conversation, but will wait until you are finished before they speak. In other countries, however, people tend to talk all at once in gatherings and meetings. The advantage of this, he jokes, is that they can have the same unproductive conversation in half the time!

I now believe that no one ever interrupts me. That is not to say that people do not occasionally speak when I am speaking. But I choose not to hear this as interruption. Instead, I choose to hear their enthusiasm about sharing something with me. I believe that perception does not shape your life; it *is* your life.

If I tell myself that you are interrupting me, I might feel irritated because my need for respect is not being met. If I understand your "interrupting" as your eagerness to give me your insight or idea, I would feel quite different. Either way, I am creating my own environment. Minute by minute, we all shape our internal environment, and from that comes the happiness or suffering of our lives. Using the tools of self-empathy and then empathy for the other allows us to hear their words not as rudeness but as an exchange we can enjoy.

But what about interrupting someone else? Is there ever a time to do that? When I was growing up, interrupting anyone at any time was strictly prohibited. So when I first heard Marshall Rosenberg speak about the importance of sometimes interrupting someone else, I was shocked. I wondered how interrupting could ever be nonviolent.

But I have shifted on this issue. Here's why. First, if I listen to you past the time I am interested or truly able to hear, I am actually disconnecting from you and doing violence to myself. Before in my life when I felt disconnected from a conversation, I pretended to listen to be polite, but I'm now sure that my eyes glazed over and the other person knew I was tuning out. Other people know when we are not present. They often respond by moving closer, speaking louder, or repeating the story. Is it really practicing ahimsa to pretend to listen when we aren't?

I have since learned to respond in another way. When I feel myself drifting away from what another is saying to me, first I tune in to myself to see what is alive in me; this involves silent self-empathy. Then I might say something like, "I'm hearing that you're excited to tell me about this, but right now there are more words than I can take in because I'm tired (assuming it is true that I am feeling tired). Can we pick another time to have this conversation when I'm predicting I'll be more able to listen?"

Another way is to first acknowledge what is going on for you at that moment. It might sound like this: "I hear that you really want to share this story with me, but I'm not able to listen fully because I'm feeling pressed for time. My husband is by the door, waiting for me to leave for an appointment, and I'm anxious about being late for it. Can we set up a time tomorrow to talk on the phone so you can finish your story? I'd love to hear it then."

Try this truth telling, and you will be amazed at how people will understand and support your predicament. Often others will be relieved by your words, because they were feeling uneasy, as they felt your attention and energy pulling away. I like this approach because it beautifully combines ahimsa, satya, and right speech. It is speech as spiritual practice.

In the long run, it is actually more loving and compassionate to speak your satya—what is alive in you—and to connect with the other person by "interrupting" than to stay silent, seemingly listening but really drifting away from them. That is not what they want, I am guessing, nor is it what you want. Speak your truth in a way designed to promote connection, and you reduce the violence you do to them, to the relationship, and of course to yourself.

## Repeating the Story

Have you ever stood and listened as a friend, coworker, or acquaintance told you the same story over and over, until you wanted to run away? Usually what happens is that they tell you about a painful incident from their past, and when your response does not meet their need for empathy, they tell it again, sometimes in a louder voice, or sometimes the next time you see them. This may be because we have been educated to think that the most important thing in the world is what other people think about us.

As speakers, we may have done this as well. We are confusing understanding and empathy. Usually we think that what we want most is to be understood by the other person, but what we probably actually want is empathy. Because we think we want to be understood, and through that understanding to experience a kind of healing, we tell the story over and over. Ironically, this strategy not only fails to satisfy our need to be understood, but it can also alienate us from the listener.

To practice spiritual speech is to hear not what someone thinks, but to hear the feelings and needs behind the words. When someone tells you what they are thinking about an experience or event, it will probably not connect them with their pain in a way that is healing. When someone tells you a story over and over, offer them your empathy by guessing what is going on with them. It might sound something like this: "When you say that, are you wanting me to get how much pain that caused you then, how much pain you are still in about it, and how much you may have been longing for respect (or clarity, or whatever it was)?"

When you offer an empathic guess as to what is going on for them at this moment, it is much more likely that they will shift into the present moment and into a connection with you. When you lead them gently into an empathic connection, you both will probably enjoy the moment more. When you do this, typically the person will stop telling the story, and you will stop pulling away.

When we speak our truth, we share what is real inside us. Then not only are we living in the present, we are also building a bridge to our authentic selves and to the authentic selves of others.

## Practicing Nonviolent Communication

### *Anger*

- Remember the last time you were angry about a small thing. Sit quietly and give yourself silent empathy about the incident, guessing with compassion what really might have been alive in you. Note how your feelings shift.
- Spend a day noticing what it takes to stimulate anger in you. Whatever those things are, you are giving them tremendous power in your life. Use self-empathy when those thoughts arise.

### *Enemy images*

- Think about someone you don't know but have enemy images about—for example, a public figure. Imagine a conversation with that person in which you give them empathy. Notice how you shift.

- The next time you have a meeting with a person or group about an issue, notice who in the room stimulates your enemy images. During the meeting, give them silent empathy.

### *Telling a story over and over*

- The next time someone repeats a story to you, notice how you pull away and how they respond to that pulling away.
- What stories do you repeat to others? What might be the unmet need that drives the retelling? When you can, give yourself empathy around it.

# 6 Talking to Our Partners

*Speak when you are angry—and you will make the best speech you'll ever regret.*

—LAURENCE J. PETER

FEW THINGS TEST our ability to be present and to grow as human beings as our most intimate relationships. Those relationships can stimulate our deepest emotions, both those we enjoy and those we don't, and can stimulate our strongly held patterns of speaking and acting. It is certainly never dull being in such a relationship. Ike and I think there should be a kind of yoga called "relationship yoga." It certainly is as challenging to relate to our partners with consistency and love over many years as it is to practice any yoga pose!

One day Ike and I were driving on a trip. I asked him what I thought was a simple question: "Are you thirsty?" He responded to the exact question asked and said, "No." My response to him was irritation. When

I tell this story in workshops, people often laugh. I believe they recognize themselves as either the questioner or the respondent.

Because of my upbringing and my beliefs, I asked Ike if he was thirsty as a way of saying that *I was thirsty*. As strange as that might sound to some readers, that was my typical pattern of asking for what I wanted. I was really trying to say, "I'm thirsty. Would you be willing to stop for some water?" But I had learned to never ask, or certainly to never ask directly, for my needs to be met. I believed that to ask for what I wanted was selfish, demanding, and not spiritual. My strategy was to use language to protect myself from what I imagined would be the other person's judgments about my needs. I disguised my needs by speaking in a way that made the need seem to be about them, not about me. Clearly, this way of operating had ramifications for all the interactions that Ike and I had.

As we learned Nonviolent Communication, things gradually changed. First, I shifted in my beliefs about my needs, and then I shifted my speech. Now I would say, "I'm thirsty. Would you be willing to stop for some water? Anyone else want water?" In this way of speaking, I am being as clear as I can about what is alive in me. Therefore I believe I am practicing *satya* and right speech as well.

Our culture fosters an assumption that many women absorb: *Women are not to have any needs.* Many men seem to absorb the teaching from the culture that *men are not to have any feelings*. Of course these rigid notions are a strategy to help people feel safe. But the irony is that we feel much safer in relationships when we are clear about our feelings and needs. This is true for two basic reasons.

First, we feel safer when our partner reveals what he is feeling, because unexpressed feelings are often received as aggression. We sense when someone is angry or upset, especially if we live with that person in an intimate relationship. So when they express their feelings in a way that we can hear, we often feel relief, even if we don't have a solution to the stimulus for their feelings.

One day our family visited another family just as that marriage was beginning to unravel. As I was unpacking my suitcase, our three children came into the bedroom, closed the door, and asked what was going on in that family, one they had known all their lives. I told them simply that what they were feeling was very likely the feeling that often prevails in homes where the partners are on the verge of separating. I was surprised at how much relief our children expressed. They felt the disturbed energy all around them and thus were reassured when someone they trusted validated their feelings.

Men are often taught to hide their vulnerability. They may have experienced shame or embarrassment in the past when they expressed their feelings, so they feel safer when they don't. In order to support your partner, especially if he is a man, you might say something like this: "I don't feel as connected to you as I like to be when you don't reveal your feelings to me" or "I feel so much safer with you when you tell me what you're feeling." We suggest that you immediately follow statements like these with a request, such as, "How do you feel hearing what I just said?"

How you respond to what your partner says next will strongly influence their willingness to reveal themselves to you in the future. We suggest that you respond with genuine appreciation for their willingness to answer, regardless of whether you like the content of the message. Your appreciation can be genuine, even if the content of the message stimulates pain in you, if you focus on the gift the person has given by revealing himself. We encourage you not to respond with a judgment about those feelings or reject them as incorrect or wrong. We can teach our partners to act in a way that they have labeled as "vulnerable" all their lives by the way we respond to any first steps they take to share their feelings with us.

Sometimes people, especially men, are taught to believe that feelings get in the way of "getting things done," so they must deny their feelings to be productive and thus worthy. But we can help our partners to realize that in the safe circle of the relationship, vulnerability and the sharing of feelings will not only be received with love, it will be celebrated.

The second thing to keep in mind about feelings

and needs in intimate relationships is this: Women may have been educated not only to not ask for their needs to be met, but often they aren't even aware of what their needs are. Sigmund Freud famously asked: "What does woman want?" Maybe women are seen as mysterious by men because they don't express or even acknowledge their needs. Maybe if women came to know their needs more clearly, they would find the courage to ask for their needs to be met in a straightforward way. Then, not only would they please their partners, but they would feel more powerful in the world.

## Becoming Santa Claus

Another important step toward using satya and right speech in our relationship is to be aware of our beliefs about our needs. If we believe that our needs are a burden to others, we will be reluctant to request that our needs be met. One way to live in truth is to be clear about what we would like. But the process of making clear requests has another layer of importance and meaning.

When we don't ask for what we want, it can reflect the unconscious belief that our needs are not important, or paradoxically that we are special or different from others and really don't need anything. This way of thinking is a form of egoism: we secretly believe that we are better than others, that our needs are minor or nonexistent, and therefore we don't need to ask others for support. Perhaps we have twisted the teachings of yoga or Buddhism to conclude that asking for support is selfish or demanding. But there is another way to be in the world.

Ike and I have learned from Marshall Rosenberg to ask this question of ourselves: What if we acted as if our requests to each other were actually giving a gift? What if you truly believed that you were not only giving your partner a gift but the best gift in the world by making a request? That gift is the opportunity for the other person to meet your needs. You are becoming Santa Claus, and they are getting a present! Believing that our needs are a burden is its own special hell. Believing that our needs are a gift is the way out of that hell.

We are not suggesting that just because you request that your need be met in a certain way that it will be. Rather, we are suggesting, first, that you can find the courage to ask, and second, that you can do so without whining or complaining. Making a request is a way of giving your partner the gift of being able to choose to give you what you want. And giving to the people we love, when it comes from deep in the heart, is one of life's greatest pleasures. If you ask from the place of "You lucky partner, you, I'm going to give you the chance to meet my needs," you have become Santa Claus.

However, if we ask for our partner to grant our request before we have expressed our feelings and needs, they will not have what they require to enjoy the process. We want to bring people to our needs first, then to our request. We want our partners to act from the belief that meeting our needs is the most wonderful thing they could be doing at the moment. There is never any demand energy around the request. When we give from that place, we shift, our partner shifts, and the world shifts toward compassion.

Imagine your partner coming to you and saying, "What can I say or do right now to make your life more wonderful?" I am guessing that you would melt with affection. The techniques of NVC are about creating the connection whereby we can all make life more wonderful for others. This helps us live the spirit of truth, and truth is rooted in love.

Please note that when we speak this way to each other, we are never doing anything *for* the other person. In fact, no one ever does anything for anyone. *We only do things to meet our own needs.* If we do anything for our partners for any other reason than to meet our own needs of contribution and support, then we are not truly giving a gift. That type of "gift" will have expectations and strings attached to it, usually unconscious ones. The other person will feel the hidden obligation. If we do anything out of "should" or "have to" energy, if there is even the slightest tinge of resentment or implied punishment for refusing to do it, we are doing violence to ourselves and to the relationship.

In the end, "self sacrifice" only makes others pay.

This form of sacrifice can be driven by thoughts of duty or obligation, it can be an attempt to buy love in order to get people to like us, or it can be motivated by our desire to please God. If we act from these motivations, we suffer and we create suffering. Instead, if everything we do for others comes from the intention of meeting our own needs, everything is clear, and we live in the present.

## Dogging for Your Needs

Remember the duck index from chapter 4? Before you give to your partner, check in with your duck index. Give to them only when it is high on your index. Don't give up asking for your needs to be met just because you are met with resistance. Dog for your needs—have the persistence of a dog that continually comes back and slips his head under your hand so you will pet him. He does it with love.

Go to your partner and tell him what you need, and make a request. If your request is not granted, give yourself and your partner silent empathy and then ask again. And again. Ask from your heart, using slightly different strategies each time. This is not the same as nagging. Nagging is a form of demand; asking for needs to be met is a request. When we nag, we are in effect acting like the other person is at fault—we "blame" them for our emotional state and so expect them to "fix" us. Asking for our needs to be met takes responsibility for what we need and attempts to get it. So make sure that no criticism is implied or expressed. All criticism is the tragic expression of unmet needs. Never forget that your needs are a gift to you and a gift to your partner, because your needs are what connect you both directly to life.

## Fighting about the Same Thing Over and Over

It seems to be a hallmark of long relationships that partners tend to have the same fight over and over again. Our fight is about temperature. One of us says, "It's cold in here," and the other one replies, "No, it isn't," and we are off to the races. Partners are often unable to resolve long-standing conflicts because when the disagreement arises, the people involved go immediately to strategies to solve the problem. We personally go to the tried-and-true, "Well, if you're cold, put on more clothes," while the other partner says, "No, if you're hot, take off some clothes." What works better is to use empathic connection around each person's feeling and needs, to make sure each person has been heard. When we feel heard, we become curious about what the other's needs are, and we are open to new strategies to meet all the needs that are up at the moment.

Marshall Rosenberg says he can help couples solve any long-standing disagreement within twenty minutes of the time that the couple have begun to hear each others needs. Years of conflict gone in twenty minutes? The key is first giving and receiving empathy. He once asked an audience to say who among the couples there had the longest-standing disagreement. A couple spoke up who had argued about the checkbook for decades. It took quite a while for each partner, with his help, to hear the other's needs empathically, but when they did, they solved the problem of the checkbook in about ten minutes.

When I heard this story, I felt great hope and yet profound sadness. We all get stuck in repetitive arguments. For me it has never been about the "topic" of the fight; it has always been about the need for empathy. Learning to give and receive empathy with our partner opens doors of connection and love. We all are longing to be seen and heard, just for who we are, without judgments. Give that gift to your partner, and maybe you will transcend your most common fight. It's worth a try.

## Going Unconscious

All spiritual practices are fundamentally about the same thing: being present and living with an open heart. It is the essence of living consciously. But in the hectic business of daily life and the habitual patterns of long relationships, almost of us "go unconscious" when our patterns are triggered by our partner or by circumstances.

It is worthwhile to spend some quiet time reflecting

on what you do when you go unconscious in your relationship. Do you withdraw? Do you blame the other? Do you defend against all incoming statements because you hear them as criticism? Once you have found the basic thought and reaction you use habitually, share it with your partner. They will definitely recognize your pattern; they have been dancing with it for years. Then try this strategy.

Agree upon a signal that your partner can use to help you in your commitment to stay present in the midst of an upset. It might be a raised finger or a certain word that your partner can use to remind you that you are lapsing into your pattern. You can choose the same signal or individual ones. The important thing is that you use them.

Some years ago, Ike discussed with our family his habitual pattern of forgetting how much he valued staying present, and he asked for us all to help him notice when he was not doing that. Soon afterward, one night at dinner he became irritated and began to speak in a critical way. One of our children, then a young adult, remembered the mutual agreement Ike had made with us and said, "Dad, is this the way you want to interact? Is this the type of connection you want to have right now?" That was enough to remind Ike of his values and commitment to clarity in communication. He said he was going to leave the room, get centered, and return to connect in the way he wanted with his son. And he did so.

The rest of our evening was pleasant for everyone, as we celebrated our time together as a family. It was a breakthrough for all of us. We learned that we *can* change our patterns, if we remain aware of what we are doing. Ike's choices were our inspiration.

## Never Hear Criticism

When we lose connection with the intention behind what we say, especially with intimate partners, we find that we have a vast vocabulary for saying what is wrong with them. Some partners hear criticism no matter what we say. What is needed is emergency empathy.

Sometimes the most efficacious thing is to say something like, "I'm not able to hear you right now. I'm going for a walk until I can get centered, and then I'd like to try again to hear what your heart wants me to hear."

Never hear what the other person *thinks* of you. They may think that you caused their pain and may even use guilt to trick you into thinking that you did indeed cause it. You didn't. It is not what the other person said that caused my pain; it is how I chose to hear it.

You may have stimulated the other person, but they created their own pain by the way they heard you. So, instead of hearing what your partner *thinks,* hear what they are saying from their heart. Hear what is hidden in the words of criticism of you. Is the other person is actually hurt, afraid, or frustrated? Give yourself and them silent empathy. Do not go to solution or strategy until you both have shifted.

One of the most pungent things we have learned from Dr. Rosenberg is that in relationships we are all "becoming progressively less stupid." Hopefully the relationship can withstand the strain until we begin to figure out how we trigger each other and which specific words do that. Then we can give and receive empathy to create connection and ease, at least until the next time.

One strategy that can strengthen connection is to consistently celebrate how the other person is enriching your life. Build that celebration into your relationship structure; create a space to do it every day. One way might be to offer appreciation to your partner for something she does every day. For example, "I really appreciate you getting up early and going to work so we can live in this house," or "Thank you for fixing this dinner. I know it took time and effort, and I want you to know that I enjoy the tastes and trust in its wholesomeness."

## The Myth of Independence

Most of us are raised to think it is important to be independent, to think for ourselves, to make up our own minds about things. Partly because of these cultural norms, we are not clear about the distinctions between dependence and independence, and therefore we miss the joy of interdependence.

To be dependent is to believe and act from the idea that only a specific other person can meet my needs—for example, my need for love. I might say something like, "I need you to love me." Actually this statement is a strategy. If we believe that in order to get love, we must get it from that specific person, then we are dependent on that person. So unless that person gives us love, or we can persuade, manipulate, or cajole them into loving us, we will not have love in life. That is a scary place to be.

To protect ourselves from this dependency and from potential hurt, sometimes we act and speak from the belief that we are completely independent of others. This way of looking at the world reinforces the idea that no one can meet our needs except ourselves. This may seem like a safer place to be, but it is a lonely place.

There is a third way to act and speak. It is to use your speech to acknowledge the interdependence we have with other people. Interdependence means that my needs cannot be met unless yours are, and yours cannot be met unless mine are. With this awareness, it becomes clear that needs, the human needs we all have, are what connect us to each other.

No relationship will thrive and be healthy unless both people are getting their needs met. This includes the relationships of boss and employee, husband and wife, teacher and student, and friends. A relationship cannot survive in which one person is consistently getting what they need and the other one is not.

## How to Enjoy Screwing Things Up

One of the things that often holds us back when we begin to use NVC with our partners is the fear of making a mess. Our advice is to go ahead and make a mess without fear. Then you can use your newly acquired NVC skills to clean up the mess. Relax with confidence in your ability to mourn your "mistakes" with your partner and to try again to create connection.

## Practicing Nonviolent Communication

### *Making life more wonderful*

- Make a plan with your partner that every day for the next week, when you wake up, the first thing you will ask each other is "What can I do to contribute to your day being more wonderful?" Notice what fun this is to do. Be sure to follow through with empathic listening to the response and with the requested action, if it is at least a 6 on your duck index.
- At the end of the day, acknowledge out loud to your partner your gratitude for what they did to make your life more wonderful today.

### *Intentional guessing*

- Spend ten minutes with your partner, and have them tell you about a recent incident (not involving you) in which they were upset. Help them recall what feelings and needs came up for them at the time.

Then support them to say how they are feeling and what they are needing in the present moment, as they recall the incident. Do not offer solutions, just empathy.

- When it feels comfortable, try this same exercise with an incident that does include you and your partner.

# 7 Talking to Our Children and Parents

*Telling someone what was wrong with them never got me what I wanted from them.*

— MARSHALL ROSENBERG

A FEW YEARS into our study of NVC, we were having a discussion with our teenage daughter. Apparently our skill level was still elementary, because when we tried to use NVC in our conversation, she replied: "I have no feelings, needs, or requests, so stop using that NVC stuff on me. I know what you're doing." Because of our lack of experience, we were effectively stymied by her response. Indeed, learning to communicate in a new way with our children and parents is probably one of the most difficult areas in which to use the principles of spiritual speech.

Perhaps one of the reasons that the child–parent relationship is challenging is that it has to do with shifting power. When children are born, we as parents seem to have all the power. Gradually, as they grow, we surrender more and more choices to them, until they leave home and live their own lives. But often parents hold the unconscious belief that they are in charge of their children, of what they say, do, and believe.

The opposite happens in the relationship with our parents. When we visit our parents, or if they have passed and we think of them, there sometimes arises the old rebellious spirit. We may feel slightly irritated in their presence if we perceive that they are judging our choices or trying to tell us what to do or offering advice. We want them to back off and treat us as the adults we believe we have become, even if we are only fifteen years old at the time.

## Power Over or Power With

Marshall Rosenberg relates that his relationship with his children shifted dramatically when he realized he could not make his children do anything—he could just make them wish they had. When he operated this way, though, he found out that they would make him wish he hadn't made them wish they had. So goes the world, when we operate from the paradigm of "power over."

As young parents, Ike and I believed that parenting was not only about loving our children, but it was also about making them mind us and act in certain ways. We believed that was what responsible parents did.

There is only one problem with acting from this belief: It is a short-term solution, and it has consequences you may not like. It is possible at times to get your child to do what you want by using your power as a parent. But there is no way that using power can force your child to do something for the reasons you want them to do it. Unless we can find other ways to connect and communicate, we will be building child–parent relationships that not only aren't satisfying but that are filled with suffering for both child and parent.

Ike and I quickly found out with our first child that we couldn't even control a two-year-old. We could put him in his room because he was having a temper tantrum and tell him to stay, but we couldn't make him like it or stop trying to come out. It was quite humbling.

Here is where speech as a spiritual practice comes in. Suzuki Roshi said, when asked about controlling teenagers, "You cannot control their behavior, you can only control your own." This makes it clear that a regular practice of self-awareness, like yoga or meditation, can help us as parents be clear about what is alive in us and what our needs are exactly. It can help us be a little more discriminating about what is in our power to change and what is not. Finally, self-awareness practices can help us to see our child as an individual and to separate clearly what are our needs and what are theirs.

I (Judith) once heard a child psychologist say that when your child is facing a difficulty, ask yourself: Is it my problem as a parent, is it the child's problem, or is it a problem for both of us to solve? He suggested that if it is your problem, you get help for it. If it is your child's problem, you support them in solving it. If it is a problem for both of you, you figure out a way to solve it together. The difficult part is discriminating whose problem it is.

It is very easy to want to do everything for our children to protect them. There is even a term for this: helicopter parent. This is the type who hovers over every activity and every aspect of their child's life, like a helicopter. It is really the manifestation of attempting to have power over the child's life and choices. It may come from desperately wanting to make the child's life happy, healthy, and safe, but it has consequences.

By learning NVC, we have shifted our understanding of power in human relationships. We learned that what we wanted was power *with* our children, not power *over*. This does not mean that we give up our role as their parents; rather it means that we understand that all human beings have power, even in the most constrained circumstances. If someone points a gun at your head and says, "Your money or your life," you may not like that choice, but you still have the power to make one.

Children, even young children, have choice about their feelings and their thoughts. They may do what we want on the outside, but they will do what they want on the inside. The most successful relationships with children are based on recognizing that they also have power. This does not mean that we give up our responsibility to protect and guide, but rather that we understand that they are part of the process. If you don't believe this, try to use your power to "make" a teenager do well in school. Let us know how it goes! They will do what they will. We can only choose our own actions. If our language does not reflect this, then we are not living in reality.

We learned in NVC that we had been acting as if we had power over our children. To act from the belief of power over is to attempt to use words or actions to get someone to do what you want them to. There is an implicit use of force behind the words if the other does not comply. If you want to see what kind of world this belief creates, look around. Even with all the progress human society has made, we often attempt to solve problems by the use of power over.

Power with, on the other hand, uses communication skills to recognize each person's power and to come to a mutually acceptable solution to problems in which all the people in the situation have their needs met.

Two examples of how we learned about the use of power with our children might be useful here. One instance was when our thirteen-year-old daughter and her friend proposed going to a rock concert and "staying out till 2 a.m." When she initially asked, my silent reaction was "in your dreams!" But recognizing that she was taller than me and could walk out the door and

I would never again see her (or any potential grandchildren), and furthermore acknowledging that I was not going to chain her to her bed, I realized that my best strategy was to negotiate. I used my favorite parenting mantra: "Oh, tell me more." This is an effective tactic that gives you time to breathe and consider the situation. I got clear during this pause that I really didn't care about her going with her friend to the rock concert, but I really cared about her being safe.

As she continued to enthuse about the groups and the music, I remembered my NVC. I said, "I hear that you're excited about the concert, but I have some concerns. Would you like to spend ten minutes now brainstorming ways that we could both get our needs met in this situation?" This type of approach acknowledges the other person's needs and passions. The other person feels heard and is then more willing to hear you and your needs.

When she agreed to continue the discussion on the needs level, I told her that my needs were all about her safety. I said that I had three strategies that would meet my need for safety and that I was guessing would also meet her needs for adventure and fun. I suggested them one by one, and she agreed to them all. These strategies were that her older and very trustworthy brother accompany them, that he stay with them so they were not roaming unaccompanied in the crowd, and that she be home by midnight.

Not only was all this agreeable to her, but we ended

the discussion with a sense of connection and celebration instead of the argument that so often happens when teenagers push the envelope and parents react with fear and power plays. The most interesting thing about the whole situation was that she came home from the concert at 10 p.m. because it was too loud. She felt free to make the choice to meet her needs. She didn't need to prove anything to me by rebelling.

Another example involved our nineteen-year-old son. He was driving alone to a ski area to join another young man who we knew, for a few days of snowboarding. As he was leaving, I tried to force an agreement from him about calling me from the road and when he arrived. He balked, and I upped the ante. "No," I said, "call me every day, just call me all the time! Never stop calling me!" I was feeling the need for reassurance and connection, and he was feeling the need for adventure and autonomy. His response, famous in the annals of teen and parent relationships was, "You don't trust me!"

Thank goodness Ike gently intervened and lent us his NVC skills. He helped our son and me get clear about our respective needs. When my son heard that me wanting "lots of phone calls" was a strategy to meet my needs for safety and reassurance, he relaxed because *it was about me and was not an implied criticism.* He began to understand that it was not about me trusting him. And when he demonstrated with words that he heard me, I relaxed and was able to hear his needs for autonomy and adventure.

When we finally heard each other's needs, we were able to agree on a phone call strategy that met both of our needs. Ironically, by the third day of the trip, I asked him to stop calling me so much, because I was content with our connection. The few minutes we had spent getting clear on our needs through NVC were about each of us paying attention first to what was alive in ourselves, then to what we really needed, and finally to being willing to let go of our respective expectations (strategies), so we could be open to outcome.

The situation resolved with connection and both of us getting our needs met. It was a great learning for me. Once again, I saw that power with my children was what I wanted, not power over them, because power with them helped to create the kind of relationship I wanted to have.

## Protective Use of Force

NVC, as well as yoga philosophy and Buddhism, all hold dearly the values of nonviolence. NVC offers the additional teaching of the protective use of force. The protective use of force means using just the force necessary to prevent someone from harming themselves or others. That force is applied with compassion and not anger, and it is never used to punish.

It is occasionally necessary to use force to protect or save lives. If my child were in the street, I would not stop and have an NVC conversation with a three-year-old about the danger of an oncoming truck. I would grab the child and run to safety. To use NVC does not imply that we surrender our protective urges as parents, or that we give in or give up our parenting responsibilities. Rather it helps us realize that most of the decisions we make regarding our children are not about life-threatening situations, and that valuing and using the tool of mutuality can make the relationship deeper and more satisfying.

A famous story from India beautifully expresses the concept of the protective use of force. A sadhu was making his yearly circuit around the villages in India. In one village, after lecturing on *ahimsa*, nonviolence, he encountered a large and aggressive snake. The snake had been terrorizing the village, but it listened intently to the teachings of the sadhu regarding nonviolence.

A year passed, and the wandering sadhu returned to the village to find the snake hiding in the bushes, skinny, battered, and bruised. When asked what had happened to him, the snake replied that he had taken the teachings of ahimsa to heart and no longer threatened anyone. The children quickly learned that the snake was not a threat and taunted and threw rocks at him. The snake was no longer able to find food and was near death.

The sadhu responded, "Yes, I did teach you to practice nonviolence, but I never told you not to hiss." Using protective force with our children, or anyone else for that matter, is remembering to hiss when necessary.

## Autonomy, Autonomy, Autonomy

One of the reasons that power over does not give us what we want is that it does not recognize or respect the fundamental requirement for a good relationship: respect for the other's autonomy. A definition of *child* or *teenager* or *young adult* might be "a person who wants you to respect their autonomy." The closer you are to the person, the more desperately they want you to respect their autonomy.

The first sign of rebellion in the child–parent relationship is often termed the terrible twos. We never understood what was so terrible about this stage of development until we were in the midst of it with our firstborn. It wasn't so terrible for him, but it was pretty terrible for us. It was the age of No! On every occasion throughout his day, for several months, he made it clear that we needed to respect his autonomy. He wanted to make the decision about when he got into the car seat and if and when he got out. He wanted to be in charge of whether he got into the bathtub and if and when he got out. He wanted to decide when he went to sleep. Child experts tell us this is a normal stage of human development. That doesn't help. I'm not sure which is more unpleasant—hearing No! all day long or witnessing the death of the illusion that we as parents have all the power.

A fascinating example of the mutuality of power between parent and child can be seen in a movie called

*One Fine Day*. The scene involves the dad (George Clooney) and his approximately eight-year-old daughter. She is under a table, clutching a kitten she passionately wants to keep, and her dad is under the table with her, just as passionately wanting her to come with him because he has a tight schedule. He tries using power over her, he tries using bribery, but nothing works until he finally begins to listen to her needs. When she feels heard, both her and his needs can be met, and she goes with him willingly. While they are not using formal NVC language, they are definitely using colloquial NVC and the spirit of mutuality.

## What We Want from Our Parents

Probably the thing we want most from our parents is their unconditional love. But following close on its heels is the desire for them to recognize and respect our autonomy. This doesn't seem to go away, even into adulthood.

As we grow up, we may feel the need to demand respect for our autonomy, and we may choose one of several strategies to get that respect. One strategy is to rebel. This is a simple and almost universal strategy: "I want X, my parents want Y, so I will do X, even though I see that Y is a better idea, because no one is going tell me what to do." This scenario is acted out daily in many homes. Sometimes the rebellion is overt and sometimes it is sneaky, but the war is on.

Another strategy is to just give up and submit to the authority of our parents. This approach can breed seething anger and hidden rebellion. It sometimes occurs in homes where rebellion may not be perceived as safe by the child, because of situations like alcoholism or abuse.

Most of us stumble through to adulthood without a clear understanding of mutuality and shared power with our parents. We may run companies, hire and fire employees, buy and sell homes, write books, and become parents ourselves, but with our parents we can still be stimulated into defending our need for respect for our autonomy.

When you find yourself in this position with your parents or grandparents, NVC would suggest that you first give yourself silent empathy for the sadness or irritation that arises when you hear your parent act in a way that does not respect your autonomy. You may need to do self-empathy frequently when you are in their presence.

You might also arrange to receive some out-loud empathy from a friend before you visit or talk with your parents. Once you are feeling full, your natural curiosity will arise about what might be alive in your parents, and you can shift to giving them empathy. When we can empathize, there is nothing to forgive, and old hurts and fears seem less important.

A final approach to create and maintain connection with your parents is to express your need and ask for specific things in return. You might say that you want to improve your communication and then guess their feelings and needs about a specific issue. Be willing to keep trying, time and again, and never stop giving yourself empathy.

## Why Approval Hurts

As parents we sometimes use our approval and praise to reward and manipulate our children. This strategy to get our needs met may seem loving, but it has problems inherent in it. When we offer approval, compliments, or praise, we are telling the other person that we like them or what they did by using evaluative language. This is to offer them our judgments, even though those judgments are usually considered to be "positive."

The problem is that implied in the praise is the unexpressed understanding that if the person did well, he could also do badly. If you look beautiful, you could also look ugly. If I put you on the "beautiful" continuum in my mind, the other end of that continuum is "ugly." Praise and compliments put your child, or any other person, in a box. It tells them who they are and therefore limits them. Think back to a time when someone gave you a compliment and you felt uneasy. Your discomfort was possibly because the compliment, even if positive, implied the possibility of its opposite.

Compliments and praise focus on extrinsic rewards.

In *Punished by Rewards*, author Alfie Kohn cites various studies that show that not only do praise and rewards fail to create the desired ends, they actually cause the desired behavior to decrease. So the long-term effect of attempting to manipulate your child or others with praise and compliments is counterproductive.

Instead of offering praise and compliments, *appreciate* your children. In NVC this means to share with others exactly what they said or did that met your specific needs. So instead of saying, "You are a good boy for washing the dishes," you might say, "When I came home and saw the clean kitchen, my needs for help and support were met. Thank you."

When we offer appreciation, we not only avoid judging others, we also reveal what contributes to our happiness and well-being. When we use NVC appreciation, we give the gift of showing another how their actions contributed to our well-being, which Marshall Rosenberg calls "the best game in town." Not only do we feel better appreciating instead of rewarding, but it has the additional advantage of connecting us to ourselves, to the other person, and to the moment. This is spiritual speech in daily life.

## Practicing Nonviolent Communication

### *Learning about power over*

- Pay attention to the language you hear on television or the radio for the next few days. Notice how often people use words that express power over others.

- Notice the next time you use words that express power over. When you can, spend some quiet time alone, connecting with how those words were stimulated at that moment by you feeling powerless.

### *Offering appreciation*

- Make a commitment to express appreciation to each of your family members once a day for a week.
- In the next conversation you have with your parents, whether on the phone or in person or in your mind, offer yourself empathy when you become agitated or upset.

# 8 Talking at Work

*Focus on what you want, not on what you fear.*
—IKE LASATER

PEOPLE OFTEN THINK of the workplace as separate from their "real" lives, and they assume a different persona and a different set of rules when they are there. I (Ike) often hear people say they feel unsafe in expressing themselves freely at work and showing who they really are. They become guarded and protected. Whether the workplace is an office, fire station, hospital or doctor's office, police station, store, or any other conceivable setting, people feel vulnerable revealing themselves, thinking that they will lose status or respect from others. For many of us, applying right speech or a particular practice such as NVC is difficult to imagine in our workplace; these fears provide obstacles, as does the simple fact that people are used to us communicating in a certain way.

When I first began to learn NVC, my workplace was a law office and the courtroom. I had been taught and I practiced certain protocol in the courtroom, and I assumed that trying anything different, such as a new way of communicating, would not only be frowned upon but might even lead to negative consequences for myself and my clients. I recall a specific situation in which I faced exactly this dilemma.

I was trying a lawsuit in federal court concerning a superfund toxic waste dump, and I was cross-examining a government witness, who was a well-qualified chemist. She had never testified in court before, and because I had taken her deposition I knew her testimony. I wanted to highlight certain parts of it to make sure it got into the court record, so in my cross-examination I was asking her questions that I knew the answers to, but I needed her to say them out loud. I was asking the questions that were more favorable to my client, while her main testimony was more favorable to the government.

This became an extremely painful process, as she would answer my question but then qualify it by restating all of her opinion that she'd already testified to. It took a great deal of time, and we were already behind in our schedule for the trial. In my frustration, I began to use all the cross-examination techniques I had learned to try to control her and get her to stop the long, duplicative explanations.

Not only did none of these techniques work, but she

began to view me (as she said to my female associate at one of the breaks) as a "sexist pig," trying to control and demean her. New as I was to NVC, it did not occur to me to try another way of communicating with her.

The cross-examination was set to continue the next day, and I was concerned that if this continued, the judge would cut off the testimony, and I would not have the complete record I wanted. As I pondered this distressing situation, a little voice in my head said, "You could try NVC." Immediately the response came: "Noooo, not in this situation!" Still I began to think about how I could language something in a way that would fit in this stilted, formal environment: me at a lectern twenty feet from the witness in the witness box, with a bunch of government lawyers all ready to object to any language I used that deviated from what they expected.

The following day, when she began to give a long explanation, I interrupted her, saying, "Excuse me." When she stopped and I had her attention, I continued, "I'm concerned about the time it's going to take to complete your testimony. I'm wondering if you'd be willing to just answer my questions and save any explanation until later. I want to assure you that you will have time to talk to government counsel before your testimony is complete, and you'll be able to explain things further if you need to. Would you be willing for now to just answer my questions?"

I must note that while I was asking this, my heart rate had skyrocketed, and I had that "heart in throat" feeling. I was panicked that someone was going to object. I was waiting for somebody to jump up and say, "You can't use NVC in the courtroom!" But nobody objected, and after looking at government counsel for confirmation, she said yes to my request. Though I had to remind her of the agreement a couple of times, she soon was self-correcting. The cross-examination proceeded much more quickly, and I got the testimony I wanted in the court record.

I offer this experience with the hope that if you feel uncomfortable using NVC in your workplace, you can rest assured that many others have faced similar fears and overcome them. If you do intend to begin practicing NVC in the workplace, first make sure that you get your need for empathy met, by naming the needs you imagine will not be met if you use NVC. You can also begin to incorporate NVC without it being obvious that you're trying something new, such as using skills silently and practicing outside the workplace, using scenarios that you experience during the day.

Self-empathy and silent empathy are both practices that can be done without anyone knowing you are doing them. With self-empathy, you are connecting with your own needs, met or unmet, and in silent empathy you are guessing the needs of other people. You can do these practices in the moment, as things are unfolding, or later, when you have a chance to reflect. You might find that your subsequent communication shifts after you have done these practices.

If you have people you trust to practice with outside the workplace, you can use role-playing to practice scenarios that are related to your work. With your role-playing partner, set up a scenario of a situation that is stimulating dissatisfaction for you, and then practice how you would like to respond to it. In this way, you can try out different options, gain facility in thinking on your feet, and practice using self-empathy and silent empathy on the fly.

While silent practices and role-playing can help you increase your skills and ease you into using NVC, you also might simply decide to start using it. Julie Greene, an NVC trainer, once told me that at a certain point she decided she was going to "jump off the cliff" and use NVC in all her interactions. She realized that she was going to create a lot of "messes" with people, but that she would use those messes as further practice. I think she meant that those who were familiar with how she communicated might experience the shift as unusual, and it would stimulate disconnection, and then she would use her skills to re-establish connection. I found that image of jumping off the cliff and using the messes as further practice very powerful. From that point on, I no longer differentiated between how I communicated in my workplace and in my private life. Since then, I have thought of work as a place to practice my yoga "off the mat."

Regardless of how and when you begin practicing right speech in the workplace, you can make your work experience more satisfactory in a number of ways. Being aware of and consciously working on requests is one of those ways.

## Requests at Work

We are generally not taught how to make requests. I sometimes jokingly say in workshops that if you ask for what you want, you're more likely to get it. This is a statement of the obvious, but often people don't feel safe enough to make requests in the workplace. They edit themselves, believing that if they reveal what they want, they will give power to the other person, and it will be used against them. While I certainly want people to be safe, being resentful and upset because needs are not getting met while at the same time not asking for what you want is a self-defeating circle.

Again, it can be helpful to work with someone outside the workplace. In practice with that person, identify the need that is not being met in the situation. When you name that need, and you feel the physiological shift in your body that says you have connected with it, you can then get clear about what strategy and request you think might meet the need. You can also role-play making that request and have the other person give you the response you fear receiving. You can then give yourself empathy and practice how you would like to respond.

As you develop more skill in making requests, you'll probably notice that others in your workplace are also not making requests. You can begin to lend your skills to others to help them make clear, doable requests. For example, if you are in a meeting and someone has been talking for a bit, you might interrupt and say, "Excuse me, Jeremy, would you be willing to tell me what you would like me to do with what you are saying? It would help me organize the information if I knew what you are wanting." This approach can help the person speaking clarify their request.

Another option would be to guess what the person might want: "Jeremy, are you telling us this because you want us to agree on a strategy to use in this situation?" Your guess may be incorrect, but again it will prompt the person speaking to tell you what they do want. Helping people reach this kind of clarity is beneficial for everyone.

In our personal lives, we often make a request directly to one person, perhaps our partner or child, but in the workplace we are more likely to be in group situations. It is important, if you are in a meeting or speaking to your work team, to be clear about not only what the request is but also whom it is directed to. Much confusion can result from meetings where either the request itself is unclear or a request is left hanging without it being directed to a particular person. In making a request, we are seeking an agreement, and there can be no agreement without another party.

Often in groups, people make demands out of their frustration with what is happening in the room. I'm sure most of us have been in situations where either we have been irritated by what is going on or someone else speaks to the room out of their own anger. When speaking out of irritation, people tend to give an analysis of what is going on and tell people to stop doing it. For instance, during a discussion someone might react by saying, "You are all just arguing. Let's get on with the real business here." In observing this happen again and again, I've noticed that these kinds of expressions, coming as they do out of frustration and not from a connection to needs, have an affect opposite to what the person is saying they want. The expression of frustration often simply triggers others to express their own irritation, and this delays the process of moving on. So what is the alternative?

I was attending a conference once, in a plenary session with about forty-five people. The facilitator asked a question of the audience that was basically asking for information to help him understand a situation related to the field. People in the audience began giving their reactions, and soon an argument developed among a number of the participants, all senior members in this conference community. This went on for about fifteen minutes, and people began to get very invested in their viewpoints.

I was feeling uncomfortable after the first few minutes and was not enjoying what was going on. The first thing I did was self-empathy. I tried to find observational language for what people were saying or doing that was stimulating me (rather than the summary judgments, "They are arguing, they are off point, they are wasting our time," which was where I started). Then I asked myself what needs of mine were not being met by what was going on. This practice was very helpful, as it created a kind of openness in me, a space that resulted from stepping outside of the judgments. I then began to look for strategies: What could I do to help in this situation that would not only meet my needs but also help other people in the room? I could have just left the room, but I had other needs that wouldn't have been met by leaving.

I stood up and interrupted, saying, "Excuse me, I'm really feeling uncomfortable with what's going on here." My saying this generated some laughter, which I attribute to the discomfort people felt hearing someone talk about their feelings in this context. I continued, "I would like to better understand what's going on and whether this is contributing to the facilitator's question. So my request is, Mr. Facilitator, would you be willing to tell us, of all that has been said in response to your question, what has been helpful to you?" The facilitator looked stunned. After a pause of thirty seconds or so, he looked at someone sitting off to the side and said, "None of it has been responsive to my question, except for what this person said over here." The comment he was referring to had come quite soon after he posed the question and was not at all on the topic of the argument. The room seemed to shift after that.

The argument stopped, and the conversation changed to the one thing the facilitator said he had found valuable. I enjoyed the ensuing conversation and found it valuable.

The shift did not occur because of my position in this community; at the time, I was one of the junior members. I think it occurred from my use of NVC to step outside of my judgments, get clear on my needs, and formulate a request that would help create what I wanted. The request, in this situation, cut through people's investment in their viewpoints and judgments of other people, returning the group to the original context—the facilitator's question.

This kind of key question can only come by stepping outside of our analyses or evaluations of what's happening and connecting with our needs. Doing self-empathy first, and then silent empathy to connect with the needs others in the group might be trying to meet by their actions, can help us be clear enough to see what we might say or do to increase the likelihood of our needs being met. If we don't do these practices first, any question we ask is more likely to come out of our frustration and will sound like some version of "Will people just shut up and move on to another topic!" When we are disconnected from ourselves, we often act in ways that create exactly what we don't want.

We tend to think we have to always be doing something outwardly in order to contribute, but I have found it powerfully effective to do nothing outwardly, while inwardly connecting constantly with my own and others' needs. Even if you are in a group situation where you don't feel comfortable speaking up, it is a real contribution to just do self-empathy and silent empathy. You change the dynamic of the meeting by doing these practices, even if you never open your mouth.

When you are just beginning to learn NVC, you might want to carry a notepad with you and do self-empathy in the notepad. Jot down observations—"Joe's been talking for three minutes on this topic"—and then identify and write down your feeling and need. When you are clear on those, see if you have a request of yourself or someone else in the group, and write that down. This informs whether you say anything in the group. Writing it down instead of trying to do it in your head might focus you more, and even if you are not able to come up with all four components, it can help you shift away from dwelling on the same old thoughts of irritation or distress. This practice shifts our being, and anything we decide to do will come from a different energy, one more likely to be in alignment with our value of right speech.

One of the primary benefits of using self-empathy and internally clarifying a request before making it is that it reduces the number of words we use. It's interesting that "efficiency" is one of the buzzwords of the workplace, yet often the concept is not extended to our communication with others. I hear people complain of interminable meetings, far too many emails containing far too many words, and irrelevant or redundant memos or voice mails. For the most part, we are not taught how to be economical in our use of words. Using NVC as a model to practice right speech has the beneficial side effect of increasing the efficiency of our communications. We can get across the most important information in a way that connects us with others, using fewer words.

People sometimes seem to talk as a way to figure out what they want to say, instead of figuring it out first and then saying it. You might find yourself in workplace situations in which someone is using more words than you as a listener are enjoying. It may be more words than the speaker is enjoying, as well. I still have the residue of a habit in which, if I had the sense that someone was not present with what I was saying, I would say more. This generally created the opposite of what I wanted; the person became even less present, and I became even more frustrated.

You can help yourself and others increase the efficiency of your communication in a number of ways. As we have said, if someone is talking more than you can take in, you can interrupt them with a question designed to help them get across what they really want to say in fewer words. If you want to say something, it helps to check with others to see if they are willing to hear what you have to say.

Often in meetings we look for a gap in conversation

and burst into that gap to try to get our point across, desperate to be heard. Sometimes we don't even wait for that gap; we cut off the last few words of the person speaking to get in our piece. But if I interrupt when another person is talking in order to be heard on my topic (instead of helping them be heard on theirs), then the other person is not going to be listening to what I say.

I increase the likelihood that I'll be heard by first making sure that they feel heard; then there is a quieting of their mind and an openness to hear something else. That openness is increased if I check with them to see if they are willing to hear my perspective. I might say, "I'd like to tell you how I'm viewing that; are you willing to listen now?" If I'm truly requesting and not demanding ("Listen to me because I listened to you!"), then they are at choice, and if they say yes, it increases the likelihood that I'll be heard in the way I would like. I suspect that the person will be more present, and I can use fewer words to get my point across. If I then want to check whether they've heard what I want them to hear or how they feel about it, I can use one of the process requests that we have discussed.

Email and the telephone are two other communication areas where efficiency can be lacking. Many people face the daily task of sorting through more emails than they can answer and reading emails that are longer than they enjoy. Reading and writing emails at work can be another component of the practice of right speech. In reading email, you can look for the four components of NVC, particularly needs and requests. If you are part of a work team where it is the custom to copy everybody on everything, this can help you know when you need to pay close attention and when you can file the email because the request is for someone else. If you find yourself irritated or dissatisfied, first connect with your own unmet need that generated the irritation. Then, guess what need the sender was seeking to meet by writing the email, to help you be more connected with what they wrote.

If the request of the email is unclear, I find it helpful to seek clarification from the sender. Just as in a meeting, getting this clarification ends up helping both you and the sender. It reduces my anxiety, because when it's clear what the person wants, then I feel freer to say whether I'm willing to do it or not, and if not, to amend the request in a way that I hope will satisfy us both.

Using NVC as a model for practicing right speech works for writing emails as well. I have practiced by writing emails that are strictly structured along the lines of my observation, my feelings about the situation, the needs I'm hoping to meet by sending the email, and a clear request. Then I rewrite the email in more colloquial language, while maintaining the clarity of the distinctions I made in the first writing. When I was first doing this practice, I found that if I tried to write colloquially without first going through the practice of making the clear distinctions, I would embed a series of judgments and conflate needs and strategies in a way that produced results I didn't like from the people I was addressing.

Telephone conversations are a large part of most people's work life, and all aspects of spoken communication apply; an additional component involves leaving voicemail messages. My practice is similar to emails. I identify ahead of time my request of the person and what information I want them to have to help them want to fulfill it. As always, doing this exercise greatly increases the efficiency of my communication. I use far fewer words, which I think is welcomed by those listening; brevity is certainly welcomed by me when I receive voicemail messages. I also tend to order the information in a voicemail differently when I think ahead. I am likely to state my request at the very beginning, followed by enough information to support the person in wanting to agree to it. If I need some information from a colleague in order to complete a proposal we are jointly working on, for instance, I might leave a message saying, "Would you be willing to call me back by the end of today with the information on _____ so I can finish the proposal?"

## Evaluations

Another reality of many people's work lives is being evaluated on their work and, if they are a manager, evaluating other people's work. Most evaluations use a scale that is applied to a series of judgments or labels, such as communication skills, teamwork, promptness in accomplishing work, and quality of work. Most of the evaluations I've seen conducted are inherently judgmental, yet they are usually couched in purportedly objective terms, which makes it difficult to know how to respond or what to do with the information. Evaluations often bring up difficult feelings, tied as they are to needs for sustainability, competence, and being understood and accepted. Assuming you cannot change the evaluation system at your workplace, how can you make evaluations more satisfying and helpful?

Since evaluations are tied to judgments about a person's actions, the key to making them more useful and less problematic is to tie them to *observations*. If you are evaluating someone else's performance, you can give examples in observation language of each area that you are evaluating. If, for example, you rated someone highly on teamwork, you could give them the specific instances in which you saw them collaborate in ways you liked. Perhaps you rated them lower on promptness of completing work, in which case you would note the three times in the last quarter when they handed in reports past the time you had anticipated receiving the reports. In making the observation, you can tie it directly to needs and make a specific request regarding improvement in that area.

If someone else evaluates you, you can lend your skills by asking them for the specific observations that would help you understand what led them to evaluate you as they did. If you are not clear on what needs of theirs are or are not met by some of the evaluation categories, you might instigate a discussion about it with them. Essentially this process translates the evaluation schema into observations and needs met or not met. And if your evaluator suggests areas of improvement but does not know how to make the requests, you can again lend your skills and translate what they say into request language.

## Gossip

Gossip is a common feature of the workplace. Gathering at the watercooler or in the lunchroom, people lower their voices to pass along a tasty tidbit they heard about someone or to share a story of what someone else did to them. Gossip is a social norm in many places, so avoiding it can be difficult, yet it is central to the Buddhist view of right speech and the yoga teaching of *satya*.

I find it helpful to define what I think is really going on when people gossip. I see two different types of gossip that serve distinct purposes. One type serves as a mechanism for developing a shared set of norms. We tell stories about other people embedded with our judgments of their conduct, and we seek agreement from the people we are telling the story to, or at least we want to see if they share our norms.

In the other type of gossip, we tell a story that happened to us as a way to meet our need for empathy. Our story of an interaction with another person expresses our dissatisfaction through our judgments of that person's conduct. We want the person listening to collude with us that we are right and the person we are talking about is wrong. The underlying dynamic here is wanting our distress in the situation to be understood and our pain to be seen. If the other person agrees with our evaluation, we get a kind of second-hand empathy, which does not truly satisfy.

We can avoid gossip by not engaging in it ourselves and also by how we respond when other people gossip to us. We can avoid instigating gossip by watching when we are drawn to repeat a story about someone else and checking for our motivation, giving ourselves empathy and then deciding how we want to proceed. When we are drawn to tell someone about a painful interaction we have had, we can recognize that what we need is empathy and find a way to get it, either through self-empathy or by working with someone familiar with NVC. If our need for empathy is met, we will not be drawn to gossip in this way.

It can be more difficult to know how to respond when others gossip to us. We might find ourselves participating simply because we don't know how to extract ourselves, or we may participate by default because we don't know what to say in response. Approached through the perspective of right speech and NVC, we can listen to the intention behind what the person is saying, looking for observations, feelings, and needs. If they are gossiping about how someone is a jerk for treating them badly, for example, rather than reinforcing their judgments, we might ask questions about what the person did that prompted that judgment, and once we've uncovered the observation, we can make guesses as to feelings and needs. I might guess that they are angry and their need for respect was not met. In this way, we help the person get their need for empathy met in a more satisfying way than agreeing with their judgments. If, on the other hand, the person is gossiping as a way to establish shared norms, perhaps telling a story about a coworker, I might guess that they want to meet their need for connection. Whether I make these guesses out loud or simply in my head, in giving empathy I act in alignment with my value of right speech and satya.

## Practicing Nonviolent Communication

### *Email and telephone*

- Choose two or three recent email messages you received. Read through them, looking for observations, feelings, needs, and requests. Write a response that carefully distinguishes those four components, and then rewrite it in more colloquial language, keeping your distinctions clear.
- Before making a phone call, think through what you

are requesting of the person and what information they need in order to want to fulfill that request. Whether you speak to the person directly or leave a voicemail, see how succinctly you can make your request.

### Gossip

- Think of a time when you felt drawn to gossip at work. What feelings and needs come up in thinking about it now? What feelings and needs do you think you were acting out of at the time?
- Notice in your workplace the next time someone engages you in gossip or you overhear gossip. Practice giving silent empathy to the person gossiping.

# 9 Talking in the World

*Those who danced were thought to be quite insane*
*by those who could not hear the music.*
—JOHN MILTON

ON SEPTEMBER 12, 2001, Ike and I had a regularly scheduled NVC practice group at our house. All the regular participants arrived, feeling a wide variety of emotions, including anger, fear, sadness, shock, hurt, and frustration. I was feeling angry about what had occurred the day before, and I stated that I could not begin to understand why it had happened. Our facilitator suggested that Ike play the role of Osama bin Laden, and I was assigned to give bin Laden empathy. As I tried to do this, I focused on guessing the needs bin Laden might have had when he chose the strategy he did for September 11.

The guessed needs that came out—the need for power and respect for his religion—were needs that I also have. When I realized this, I felt my anger disappearing and instead I felt compassion arising in me. I could connect with another human being on the level of needs, even while I totally disagreed with his actions. Please understand, I believed then and believe now that the strategy Osama bin Laden chose was unacceptable in the extreme and furthermore that he should be held accountable for that choice by spending the rest of his life in prison. But I found that I could hold that belief *without hating him.*

In fact, I understood that if I hated him, then I was no different than he was for hating my beliefs and culture. Buddha said it best: Hate never dispels hate; only love dispels hate. The irony was that if I hated bin Laden, I was contributing to the very suffering in the world that I said I was so committed to alleviating.

Some years ago, we had a direct experience of how powerful conscious speech can be in the world. One Sunday, Ike and I and a longtime friend were walking toward church in a neighborhood where a number of people were asking passersby for money. One such person approached Ike. This man was as tall as Ike (about six feet five) and was acting in a way that we defined as aggressive.

Ike and I had talked many times about what we would do in case something like this happened. So, according to our agreement, I took our friend, a four feet ten woman, and myself across the street to safety, so Ike could deal with the man without worrying about us. I quickly turned around to watch what was happening and dialed 911 on my cell phone without pushing "send." While I could not hear any words spoken, I was able to see clearly the body language of both my husband and the man.

The man was leaning in toward Ike, eye to eye, and was asking, I later learned from Ike, for money. Ike often gives money to people on the street, but he remembers that he did not want to give any money to this man, coming as it was from what he interpreted as a "demand" energy. At this point Ike remembered that he had the tool of NVC. He said something like, "I'm feeling afraid with you so close; would be willing to step back?" The man moved back and asked again, with one of his clenched hands thrust forward at about waist level. In response, Ike began to give the man empathy about the "guessed" need to be respected and to be seen and heard. After this second round, the man leaned farther back.

A third request for money was met with more empathy, and this third time the man leaned back even more, so he was standing in the yoga asana Tadasana (Mountain Pose), which is standing with awareness in a perfect vertical line. I observed this alignment and closed my phone, my fear for Ike's safety melting away. When one is centered in Tadasana, there is no aggressive urge; one is fully present.

A fourth round of empathy followed. After Ike gave this empathy, the man leaned over and put his head on

Ike's shoulder, with tears in his eyes. Only then did Ike offer the man money. Ike felt he had now "chosen" to give the money and was not being coerced. Thus both Ike's needs and the man's needs appeared to be met at that moment.

The interaction had begun as a potentially violent situation and had ended within a couple of minutes with connection and compassion. This incident cemented in me my dedication to learning and practicing compassionate communication for myself, my family, and the world. Ike and I still remember this incident with gratitude.

## Celebrating and Mourning

One of the most important aspects of using NVC in the world is to learn to mourn with awareness. Too often when we do or say something we later regret, we silently berate ourselves. This energy is not lost; it spills over into the world and into our work.

NVC suggests that when you realize you have done what you don't enjoy or feel that you have contributed to the suffering of another person, that you then mourn in the following way. Give yourself empathy for what you did or said. Use the training wheels process of observations, feelings, and needs. Guess what needs you were trying to meet by the strategy you chose.

Then you may want to address the other person or the group involved in this way: "When I think about what I said yesterday, I feel sad and uncomfortable, because my need to contribute to your well-being (or the well-being of the world) was not met." You may want to add: "I would like to commit now to trying to do it differently next time." As always, follow this statement with a specific request.

This way of stating what is alive in you is not about feeling guilty or punishing yourself. Rather it is about acknowledging what you did and what the consequences were and being willing to try it differently next time. One of the mantras I (Judith) often use after I have mourned in NVC is: How human of me! When I say this to myself, it stimulates me to remember to hold myself with compassion and forgiveness.

On the other hand, we often fail to celebrate our victories, either personally or within our families and groups. Celebrating is such fun. When you want to celebrate with awareness, you might say something like, "When I think about how the decision we made in the meeting turned out, I feel happy, because my needs for cooperation and connection were met." I think it is even better to start your expression with, "I would like to celebrate what just happened." Then offer your observations, feelings, and which needs of yours were met. You will be surprised at how much people enjoy celebrating, as opposed to bragging, and how often people will receive your mourning more deeply than if you had just said, "I'm sorry."

We both believe that mourning and celebrating are

crucial components of spreading NVC in the world. Sharing mourning and celebration connects you to others and will soothe your soul when the weight of working for social change becomes too much.

## Bringing an NVC Consciousness to the World

Practicing NVC to effect social change in the world is one of the most challenging ways we can use this communication model. While there is a great need for this work, it can be exhausting and draining in the extreme unless one receives empathy regularly and, we believe, unless one has a regular practice such as meditation or yoga to replenish the body, mind, and soul.

Sometimes we are torn between the conflicting needs to contribute to the world and to protect ourselves from the hurt that we might feel if we fail in our dreams. A story illuminates this predicament. I first heard it in a workshop with Marshall Rosenberg. As I remember it, a man was standing by the bank of a river and noticed a baby floating by. He hurriedly pulled the baby to safety, and as he did, he noticed another and another and another, until the river was full of babies floating by to certain death. He was torn between staying where he was to save as many as he could and instead running upstream to see who was putting all the babies in the river and stopping the process at its root. This illustrates the dilemma many people feel: Do I help the individual next to me in immediate need, or do I work to change the systems that create his suffering in the first place?

While there is no easy answer, our belief is that we can do both. In order to create the kind of world we want to live in and leave to generations to come, we need to help the suffering person who may be near us, beginning with ourselves. Additionally, we need to contribute to changing the beliefs and systems that create that suffering in the first place. However and wherever we decide to spend our energy, our talk and our actions will be more effective if we start with self-awareness. Spiritual speech is a tool for creating this awareness, and as such it offers great hope to us and we hope to you as well.

## Practicing Nonviolent Communication

### *Mourning*

- Think about something you said or did in the last couple of weeks that you regret. Mourn it by giving yourself silent empathy for the needs you were trying to meet when you chose the strategy you did. You may need to do this more than once.
- Once you have given yourself empathy, speak to the other person and express your mourning to them. Tell them what you feel when you think about your choices, and then be sure to include the statement

that you are committed to doing it differently the next time.

*Celebrating*

- Think of something you said or did in the last couple of weeks that you want to celebrate. Find a loved one or friend, and state this celebration out loud. Be sure to use observations, feelings, and needs when you do.
- Ask a friend or loved one to share a celebration with you. Help them by giving them empathy for their needs that were met.

# Resources

*Seek not, my soul, the life of the immortals; but enjoy to the full the resources that are within thy reach.*

— PINDAR

JUDITH HANSON LASATER
www.judithlasater.com
www.restorativeyogateachers.com

IKE K. LASATER
www.wordsthatwork.us

## RECOMMENDED READING

Peter Harvey, *An Introduction to Buddhism: Teachings, History, and Practices* (Cambridge, UK: Cambridge University Press, 1990)

Ramamurti S. Mishra, M.D., and Shri Brahmananda Sarasvati, *The Textbook of Yoga Psychology: The Definitive*

*Translation and Interpretation of Pataanjali's Yoga Sutras* (New York: Baba Bhagavandas Publication Trust, 1997)

Swami Prabhavananda and Christopher Isherwood, *How to Know God: The Yoga Aphorisms of Patanjali* (Hollywood, CA: Vedanta Press, 2007)

Alistair Shearer, *The Yoga Sutras of Patanjali* (New York: Harmony/Bell Tower, 2002)

## ORGANIZATIONS

***Center for Nonviolent Communication***
5600 San Francisco Rd. NE, Suite A
Albuquerque, NM 87109
(505) 244-4041
(505) 247-0414 (fax)
www.cnvc.org

The Center for Nonviolent Communication (CNVC) is a global organization whose vision is a world where all people are meeting their needs and resolving their conflicts peacefully. In this vision, people are using Nonviolent Communication (NVC) to create and participate in networks of worldwide life-serving systems in economics, education, justice, healthcare, and peace keeping.

The mission of CNVC is to contribute to this vision by facilitating the creation of life-serving systems within ourselves, interpersonally, and within organizations. We do this by living and teaching Nonviolent Communication.

CNVC's aim is to provide ideas, experience, and support for the living of Nonviolent Communication in community. This is accomplished by providing Nonviolent Communication training, materials, organizational consulting, and projects that develop harmonious and effective relationships.

Visit the website for information about books, CDs, and national and international trainings and workshops.

***Bay Area Nonviolent Communication***

55 Santa Clara Ave., Suite 203
Oakland, CA 94610
(510) 433-0700
(866) 422-9682 (toll free outside the San Francisco Bay Area but within the United States)
(510) 452-3900 (fax)
www.baynvc.org

The mission of Bay Area Nonviolent Communication (BayNVC) is to create a world where everyone's needs matter and people have the skills to make peace. Check the website for workshops and trainings in the San Francisco Bay Area.

# About the Authors

## Judith Hanson Lasater

A yoga teacher since 1971, Judith Hanson Lasater holds a bachelor of science degree in physical therapy from the University of California, San Francisco, as well as a doctorate in East–West psychology from the California Institute of Integral Studies. In 1974 she helped found the Institute for Yoga Teacher Education (now the Iyengar Institute of San Francisco), a nationally known yoga teacher training program that has since trained thousands of teachers. In 1975 she cofounded *Yoga Journal* magazine.

Judith modeled yoga poses for *Yoga Journal* and started and served on its editorial advisory board. She created and wrote the asana column in the magazine for thirteen years, as well as dozens of other articles relating to postures, anatomy, kinesiology, yoga therapeutics, breathing exercises, and the psychology and philosophy of yoga. She continues to contribute articles and interviews for *Yoga Journal* as a nationally recognized authority on yoga and serves on the magazine's advisory board.

She is president of the California Yoga Teachers Association, the oldest independent professional yoga teachers' association in the United States.

Judith is the author of *Relax and Renew* (1995), *Living Your Yoga* (2000), *30 Essential Yoga Poses* (2003), *Yoga for Pregnancy* (2004), *Yoga Abs* (2005), *A Year of Living Your Yoga* (2006), and *Yogabody* (2009), all from Rodmell Press. *What We Say Matters* is the first book that she and Ike K. Lasater have written together.

Judith teaches yoga throughout the world and lives in the San Francisco Bay Area.

## Ike K. Lasater

Ike Lasater facilitates the resolution of conflicts, coaches people in conflict, and teaches these skills to others. His mediation work is based on the principles of Nonviolent Communication (NVC), a communication model developed by Marshall Rosenberg, with whom Ike has done most of his formal NVC training. Ike has facilitated NVC and NVC Mediation workshops across the United States and in Australia, Hungry, New Zealand, Pakistan, Poland, and Sri Lanka. He has served as a board member of a number of organizations, including the Center for Nonviolent Communication and the Association for Dispute Resolution of Northern California. He cofounded *Yoga Journal* magazine.

Ike engaged in civil trial practice in the San Francisco financial district for twenty years. He cofounded Banchero & Lasater, a twenty-person law firm specializing in complex, multiparty, commercial, and environmental cases. He has served as member of the Mediation Panel for the United States District Court for the Northern District of California since 2001.

Ike is the author of *Words That Work in Business* (PuddleDancer Press). His experience in conflict resolution includes almost four decades of marriage and parenting of three now-adult children (who seem to enjoy interacting with their parents), long-term practice of aikido, Zen meditation, and yoga, and integrating NVC into his daily life since 1996.

# From the Publisher

RODMELL PRESS publishes books on yoga, Buddhism, aikido, and Taoism. In the Bhagavadgita it is written, "Yoga is skill in action." It is our hope that our books will help individuals develop a more skillful practice—one that brings peace to their daily lives and to the earth. We thank all those whose support, encouragement, and practical advice sustain us in our efforts.

***Catalog Request***

(510) 841-3123 or (800) 841-3123

(510) 841-3123 (fax)

info@rodmellpress.com ▾ www.rodmellpress.com

***Trade Sales/United States, International***

Publishers Group West

(800) 788-3123

(510) 528-5511 (sales fax)

info@pgw.com ▾ www.pgw.com

***Foreign Language and Book Club Rights***

Linda Cogozzo, Publisher

(510) 841-3123

linda@rodmellpress.com

www.rodmellpress.com

# Index

action requests, 46–49, 52. *See also* requests
ahimsa. *See* nonharming
anger, 71–76, 82, 137–138
apologizing, 140–141
appreciation, 114, 115
arguments, 17–19, 93–94
Arya, Usharbudh, 69
autonomy, 110–111

babies, 2, 23, 64, 142
Bay Area Nonviolent Communication, 147
beliefs, 10, 18
bin Laden, Osama, 137–138
Buber, Martin, 69
Buddhism
  beliefs avoided in, 18
  eightfold path of, 8–9
  empty rowboat tale, 75
  on hate vs. love, 138
  inquiry in, 16
  nonviolence in, 108
  speech in, 3, 9
burdens, needs vs., 64, 89
Byrom, Thomas, 18

celebrating, 97, 141–142, 144
Center for Nonviolent Communication (CNVC), 146–147
children
  appreciating, 114, 115
  autonomy of, 110–111
  babies, 23, 64, 142
  choice open to, 104
  NVC challenges with, 101–102
  power over vs. power with, 102–108, 114–115
  power shifts with, 101–102
  praise of, 113–114
  protective use of force with, 108–109
  taught to deny needs, 14–15
choice
  children having, 104
  requests as offers of, 48–49, 90
  of thoughts, 66
circle of judgment, 58
communication choices
  giving empathy, 40–46
  requests, 46–51
  self-empathy, 36–38

communication choices (*continued*)
self-expression, 39–40
table summarizing, 52
complaints, as needs, 15
connecting with oneself
central to NVC, 31
before others, 14
power of, 14
shift after, 15–16
signs of, 38
connecting with others
central to NVC, 30–31
intention for, 40, 41
by interrupting, 80
criticism, 96–97
curiosity, 38

demands, 27–28, 48, 59
dependence, 97–98
*The Dhammapada*, 18
dogging for needs, 92–93
duck index, 57, 60–64, 67

email, 129–131, 135
emotional DNA, 37
empathy. *See* giving empathy; self-empathy; silent empathy
empty rowboat story, 75
enemy images, 76–77, 82–83
evaluations, 131–133

facts, 17
feelings
under anger, 71–73
anger, 71–76
attending to, 20–21
expressing before requests, 90–91
expressing to parents, 113
identifying (table), 32
involving another, avoiding, 22–23
judgment-based, 71–72
love as need vs., 25
feelings (*continued*)
men and, 60, 86–88
with met and unmet needs, 20
not due to others, 21
NVC concepts, 20–23, 29
opinions vs., 21–22, 30
practicing, 31
in relationships, 87–89
safe to reveal, 87–88
as signals from the unconscious, 20–21
in training sentence, 22, 25–26, 28
unique to person, 21
women and, 60
Feuerstein, Georg, 8
force, protective use of, 108–109

gifts, needs as, 64, 90–91
giving empathy. *See also* connecting with others; silent empathy
aloud, 41–42
argument ended by, 94
beggar story, 138–140
to bin Laden, 137–138
focus of (table), 52
interruption and, 78, 79–80
in Pakistan, 42–46
practicing, 54
for repeated stories, 81–82
self-empathy from, 40–41
shift from, 40–41
sympathy vs., 42
training sentence for, 41
when negotiating needs, 63
gossip, 9, 133–135, 136
Greene, Julie, 121
groups at work, 123–127

Hafeez, Abdula, 42–43
Harvey, Peter, 145
hate, 137–138
*How to Know God*, 146

independence, myth of, 97–98
inquiry, 15–16
intention
  clarified by NVC, 16
  to connect, 30, 40, 41
  as focus of NVC, 14
  of request as choice, 48
  in right speech, 9
interdependence, 98
interrupting, 78–80, 128–129
*An Introduction to Buddhism*, 145
Isherwood, Christopher, 146

James, William, 35, 66
judgments
  about judging, 58
  acting in fear of, 60
  arguments from, 17–19
  enemy images, 76–77
  feelings due to, 71–72
  gossip, 133–134, 135
  moral vs. evaluative, 19–20
  observations vs., 17–19, 30, 132
  opinions, 21–22, 30
  praise and, 66, 113
  requests heard as, 40
  work evaluations, 131–132

Lasater, Ike K., 145, 150–151
Lasater, Judith Hanson, 145, 149–150
*Life Strategies*, 3
love, as need, 25

Max-Neef, Manfred, 24
McGraw, Phillip, 3
meditation, 4, 72, 103
men, feelings and, 60, 86–88
Milton, John, 137
Mishra, Ramamurti S., 145
mourning, 140–142, 143–144
myth of independence, 97–98

needs
  of babies, 2, 23, 64
  burdens vs., 64, 89
  central to NVC, 30–31
  change with time, 62–63
  children taught to deny, 14–15
  complaints as, 15
  connecting to yours, 14, 15–16
  demands vs., 59
  denying, 59, 89–90
  dependence vs., 97–98
  dogging for, 92–93
  in enemy images, 77
  expressing before requests, 90–91
  expressing to parents, 112–113
  as gifts, 64, 90–91
  in groups, 126–127
  humanness and, 23–24
  identifying (table), 33
  as life energy, 59
  men in touch with, 60
  met, appreciating, 114
  neediness, 23, 58–59
  negotiating, 61, 62–64
  NVC concepts, 23–26, 29
  practicing, 34
  in relationships, 85–86, 88–93
  responding to, 15
  in self-empathy, 37–38
  signs of met or unmet, 20
  sought by reaction, 15
  strategies vs., 24–25, 30, 61–62
  in training sentence, 25–26, 28
  types of, 23
  universal, 24
  women and, 58–59, 60, 86, 89–90
nonharming (ahimsa)
  enemy images and, 77

nonharming (*continued*)
satya and, 8, 69–70
snake story, 109
yoga teachings on, 3, 7, 69–70, 108
Nonviolent Communication (NVC)
basic concepts, 17–31
benefits for satya and right speech, 9–12
central precept, 30–31
components (table), 29
efficiency improved by, 127–128, 129–130
intention and, 14, 16
learning period for, 1–2
power of, 9–12
practice exercises, 31, 34, 51, 53–55, 82–83, 99–100, 114–115, 135–136, 143–144
practice needed for, 40
protective force in, 108–109
role-playing, 121, 122
shift for, 5, 35–36
syntax in, 14
tips for learning, 5–6
training sentence, 22, 25–26, 28, 30, 35–39, 41
in the world, 142–143
norms, shared, 133, 135

observations
judgments vs., 17–19, 30, 132
NVC concepts, 17–20, 29
practicing, 31
in self-empathy, 37
in self-expression, 39
as spiritual speech, 19
in training sentence, 22, 25–26, 28
in work evaluations, 132–133
*One Fine Day* (movie), 111
opinions, 21–22, 30
organizations, 146–147

parenting. *See* children
parents, 101–102, 111–113
Peter, Laurence J., 85
Pindar, 145
please, 64–66, 67
Prabhavananda, Swami, 146
praise, 64, 66, 113–114
pramana, 17
present, the, 26, 27, 94–96
process requests, 49–51, 52. *See also* requests
protecting children, 104, 108–109
pseudo facts, 17
Publilius Syrus, 1

reacting, 15
recommended reading, 145–146
reflection, requests for, 50–51, 52
relationships. *See also* children; work
becoming Santa Claus in, 89–92
celebrating, 97
criticism in, 96–97
dogging for needs in, 92–93
enjoying screwing up, 99
feelings in, 87–89
hearing the heart, 96–97
long-standing arguments, 93–94
myth of independence, 97–98
needs in, 61, 62–64, 85–86, 88–93
with parents, 101–102, 111–113
practicing NVC in, 99–100

realtionships (*continued*)
separating needs from strategies in, 25
unconsciousness in, 94–96
repeated stories, 80–82, 83
requests
about present, 26, 27
action, 46–49, 52
characteristics of, 26
demands vs., 27–28, 48
difficulties making, 26
doable, 26–27
in email, 130
as gifts, 90–91
in groups, 123–127
helping others make, 123
judgment heard in, 40
NVC concepts, 26–28, 29
as offers of choice, 48–49, 90
practicing, 34, 54–55
process, 49–51, 52
reluctance to make, 64
after self-expression, 39
in training sentence, 28
translating others' speech into, 64–66
types of, 46–51, 52
in voicemail, 131
at work, 122–131, 133
response
to gossip, 134–135
reaction vs., 15
requests for, 49–50, 52
right speech. *See also* satya (truth); spiritual speech
about ourselves, 36
ahimsa and, 69–70
in Buddhism, 3, 9
defined, 9
difficulties of, 9
for email, 129–131
interrupting in, 78–80
NVC benefits for, 9–12
spiritual speech as, 35
righteous anger, 74–76
Rodmell Press, 153–154
Rosenberg, Marshall
on appreciation, 114
arguments ended by, 93–94
on children, 102
on criticism, 101
duck statement of, 57
on interrupting, 78, 79
Judith's first seminar with, 13, 15
Max-Neef's work used by, 24
on requests as gifts, 90
on spiritual speech, 70–71
on stupidity, 97

Safire, William, 7
Santa Claus, 89–92
Sarasvati, Shri Brahmananda, 145
satya (truth). *See also* right speech; spiritual speech
ahimsa and, 8, 69–70
alive in one, 70
in giving empathy, 41–42
NVC benefits for, 9–12
spiritual speech as, 35
when interrupting, 79–80
in yoga, 3, 7–8
screwing up, 99
self-awareness, 70, 103, 140–141
self-empathy. *See also* connecting with oneself
for anger, 72–74
curiosity with, 38
efficiency of, 127–128
for enemy images, 76–77
energetic shift with, 38, 73
focus of (table), 52
from giving empathy, 40–41
for gossip avoidance, 134
in group situations, 126, 127–128
for mourning, 140

self-empathy (*continued*)
notepad for, 127
practicing, 51, 53
role-playing, 121, 122
social change and, 76
toward parents, 112
training sentence for, 37–38
when interrupted, 78
when interrupting, 79–80
at work, 120, 121, 122, 126, 127–128
self-expression
focus of (table), 52
practicing, 53–54
training sentence for, 39
Shearer, Alistair, 146
"should" energy, 91–92
silent empathy. *See also* connecting with others; giving empathy; self-empathy
effectiveness of, 40–41
for enemy images, 76–77, 82–83
focus of (table), 52
in group situations, 126, 127
role-playing, 121
at work, 120, 121, 126, 127
social change, 74–76, 142–143
spiritual needs, 23
spiritual practice, 4–5, 16, 20–21, 94
spiritual speech, 19, 35, 70–71. *See also* right speech; satya (truth)
strategies, needs vs., 24–25, 30, 61–62
Suzuki Roshi, 103
sympathy, 42
syntax, 14, 28, 35–36

telephone, 131, 135–136
*The Textbook of Yoga Psychology*, 145–146
thank you, 64, 66, 67, 97
thoughts, 10, 66
training wheels sentence
distinctions embedded in, 30
for giving empathy, 41
moving beyond, 30
overview, 22, 25–26, 28
practicing, 28, 30
for self-empathy, 37–38
for self-expression, 39
shift for, 35–36
translating others' speech, 64–66, 67
truth. *See* satya

unconsciousness in relationships, 94–96

van der Post, Laurens, 57
Veda, Swami, 69, 70
violence, 59, 80
voicemail, 131, 136

women, needs and, 58–59, 60, 86, 89–90
work
efficiency at, 127–128, 129–130
email, 129–131, 135
evaluations, 131–133
fears about NVC at, 117–120, 121, 122
gossip, 133–135, 136
groups at, 123–127
interrupting at, 128–129
requests at, 122–131
role-playing, 121, 122
shift at, 120, 121, 122, 126, 127
silent practices, 120, 121
telephone, 131, 135–136
vulnerability at, 117, 122
world
bringing NVC to, 142–143
run by beliefs, 10

world (*continued*)
social change, 74–76, 142–143

yoga
asana and right speech, 4
inquiry in, 16
nonviolence as value of, 3, 7, 69–70, 108
yoga (*continued*)
self-awareness from, 103
teachings on satya, 3, 7–8, 69–70
Yoga Sutra of Patanjali, 2–3, 7–8, 17, 69–70, 146
*The Yoga Sutras of Patanjali*, 146
*The Yoga-Sutra of Patanjali*, 8